The Dictionary of Political-Operational Work

Also known as

The Stasi Dictionary

(Abridged Edition)

Ricky Bennison

The Dictionary of Political-Operational Work

Also known as

The Stasi Dictionary

(Abridged Edition)

Edited by Ricky Bennison MA PGCE

Translated by the HyperHat company

Copyright © Ricky Bennison 2024

The moral rights of the author have been asserted

Published by Robin Publishing

ISBN: 978-0-9933963-8-0

Dedicated to the writer Jurgen Fuchs and all the victims
of decomposition methods,
past and present.

*We must be free not because we claim freedom,
but because we practice it.*

~ William Faulkner

A Note on this Abridged Version

This version is a little under half the length of the full dictionary, with a corresponding reduction in the number of definitions given. Some entries have links (represented by an arrow symbol or the words 'see also') to other entries which relate to associated information. What these links would ordinarily connect to may not be present in this abridged version.

Explanation of Acronyms and Abbreviations

The acronyms used in this translation are based upon the original German spelling. For example, DDR (Deutsche Demokratische Republik) is used instead of GDR (German Democratic Republic). There is an Abbreviation and Acronym Guide at the back of the dictionary which lists them all, what they decompress to in the German, and their respective English translations.

Among the most important acronyms in the dictionary are:

MfS- Ministerium für Staatsicherheit. Which translates to Ministry for State Security. This was the state security and secret police service of the DDR i.e. the Stasi.

IM- Inoffizieller Mitabeiter. Which translates to Unofficial Collaborator. This was a member of the East German population who collaborated with the Stasi in terms of surveillance, operational decomposition, or in some other manner.

Chekist- this is both an abbreviation and a colloquialism. It is a reference to the historical communist secret police, the Cheka, who the Stasi traced their lineage from. As it is used in the dictionary, it generally refers to the Stasi but can also refer more widely to other groups and organizations who claimed a similar lineage, such as the KGB.

Contents

Abduction 1

Abduction of Persons 1

Ability to Testify 2

Ability, operative 2

Act of Treason 3

Action, Operationally Significant 4

Action, Operative 4

Agent Conservation 4

gent Provocateur 5

Agent Radio Operator 5

Agent Shutdown 5

Agent Smuggling 5

Agent Training 6

Agent-Handling Office 6

Aircraft hijacking 6

Alternative Legend 7

Analysis of Person Movements 7

Analytical Work 8

Analytical Work; Methods 9

Annual Plan of Political-Operative Work 9

Anti-Constitutional Conspiracy 10

Antisocial Behavior 10

Anti-State Activity 11

Archiving	11
Arrest, preliminary	12
Asociality	13
Assassination	15
Assessment of the Political-Operational Situation	15
Asylum Request	16
Attacks Against the Ministry for State Security (MfS)	17
Attitude	18
Attitude Analysis	19
Attitude Formation	20
Attitudes towards the MfS	21
Authorization System	21
Behavior Disorder	23
Border Area	25
Border Provocation	25
Border Security Forces	27
Border Violation	27
Breach of Duty	28
Bringing in	28
Cadre Reserve	29
Case Processing	30
Centers of Political-Ideological Subversion	31
Central Enemy Object Case (ZFOV)	32
Central Operational Case (ZOV)	33
Central Person Database (ZPDB)	34
Chain of Circumstantial Evidence	34
Chekist Personality	35

Churches; Misuse of	36
Circumstantial Evidence	37
Complex Assignment	38
Compromising Material	38
Conflict	40
Confrontation	40
Contact Ability	41
Control	41
Corruption	42
Counteraction	42
Counterintelligence Work, Politically-Operative	43
Counterrevolution	45
Counter-Terrorism	46
Covert Apartment	47
Crime	48
Crime; Relationship to Subversion	48
Criminal Human Trafficking Group; Smuggling Methods	49
Criminal Procedural Coercive Measure	49
Criminalistic Traces	51
Cross-Border Traffic; Exit Ban	51
Cross-Border Traffic; Misuse Actions in Entry and Transit Traffic	53
Data Protection	54
Deconspiracy	55
Demonstrative Offenders	55
Demonstrative-Provocative Behavior	56
Depth Security	57
Diplomatic Representations and Privileged Persons; Protection	58

Disinformation	60
Dissident	61
Document Examination	61
Double Agent	63
Eastern Research	65
Economic Disruption Activities	67
Electronic Warfare	69
Encryption	69
Enemy	69
Enemy Band	70
Enemy Manipulation	70
Enemy object	72
Enforcement of State Authority	72
Espionage	74
Evidence Collection	76
Expert IM	78
Expertise	78
Fingerprinting	79
Foreign flag	80
Full-time Security Officers	80
Grid	81
Group Analysis, Operational	82
Habits	83
Hatred	84
Hostile activity; camouflage of	84
Hostile activity; combating of	85
Hostile Agents	86

Hostile Attitude	86
Hostile Group; Extraction of Persons	86
Identification Features	88
Identification, Criminalistic	88
Ideological Base	89
Image of the enemy, Chekist	89
Imagination	90
Imperialist Human Rights Demagoguery	91
Imperialist Intelligence Services	92
Imperialist Intelligence Services; Working Method	95
Imperialist Mass Media	97
Incident Investigation; Preparedness	98
Incitement	99
Inciting Slogan, Anti-State	99
Individual Interests	99
Infiltrator	100
Influence	101
Information Flow	101
Information Gathering	102
Instructor Connection	103
Intelligence Contacting	103
Intelligence Evaluation of Failures	104
Intelligence Misuse	104
Intelligence Recognition Meeting	105
Interference	105
Internal Security of the Ministry for State Security (MfS)	108
Interrogation of Suspects	110

- Investigation Planning 111
- Investigative Work 112
- Investigative Work; Means and Methods 115
- Justified Risk Action 116
- Latency of Hostile Activity 116
- Leading Question 117
- Leisure area 118
- Lie Detector 118
- Line Principle 119
- Long-Term Conceptions 119
- Loyalty 120
- Main Task of the MfS 121
- Mass Psychological State, Operationally Significant 122
- Meeting 123
- Meeting Conduct 123
- Members of the MfS 124
- Members of the MfS; Recruitment 124
- Members of the MfS; Requirement Profile 125
- Microdot 125
- Military Inspection (MI) 126
- Misuse of Art and Culture 128
- Motivation for Operational Actions 128
- Negative Attitude 128
- Negative Grouping 129
- Nonviolent Uprising 129
- Object Security 130
- Objectivity of Political-Operative Work 131

Observation Ability	131
Odor Differentiation	132
Offender's Personality	132
Operational Adaptability	134
Operational Base	135
Operational Combination	135
Operational Decomposition	136
Operational Immediate Measures	137
Operational Investigation	138
Operational Liaison System	139
Operational Marking	140
Operational Method	141
Operational People Skills	142
Operational Situation	143
Operational Tactics	143
Operationally Significant Clues	144
Operationally Significant Incident	145
Operationally Significant Mass Psychological Condition	146
Operative Forces	147
Operative Forces; Behavioral Line	147
Operative Person Control (OPK)	148
Operative Process (OV); Conclusion	149
Operative Process (OV); Introduction of IM	151
Oral Incitement, Anti-State	152
Person Hideout	152
Person Identification	153
Perspective Cadre	154

Planning of Political-Operative Work	154
Political Underground Activity	156
Political Underground Activity; Precursors	156
Political-Ideological Subversion	158
Politically-Operative Reconnaissance Work	159
Politically-Operative Work	160
Political-Operative Conspiracy	162
Political-Operative Vigilance	163
Prejudice	164
Prevention	165
Preventive Conversation with Youths	167
Public Relations	168
Quarters for Negatively Decadent Youth	169
Ranger	170
Recovery	170
Recruitment Proposal	171
Registration	172
Relationship of Trust	172
Relocation of IM	173
Reporting System	173
Re-Recruitment	174
Responsiveness	175
Return Connection	176
Revanchist Organizations	176
Revelation of Suspects to Unofficial Collaborators (IMs)	177
Riot	178
Rules of Political-Operative Conspiracy	178

Rumor	179
Sabotage	180
Sanction	181
Secrecy Holder	181
Secret Intelligence Liaison System	182
Security	183
Security Forces	184
Self-Reporter	184
Single Leadership	185
Skill, operative	185
Social Employee for Security (GMS)	186
Social Harmfulness	186
Socialist Economic Integration; Political-Operative Security	187
Socialist Security Policy	189
Source	191
State Demonstrative Measures	192
Subversion	192
System, hostile search	195
Tension Indicators	196
Territorial Principle	197
Terror	197
Terrorism	198
Tipper	201
Unofficial Collaborator (IM)	201
Unofficial Collaborator (IM) Candidate; Recruitment Conversation	202
Unofficial Collaborator (IM) of the Defense with Enemy Contact or for Direct Processing of Persons Suspected of Enemy Activity (IMB)	203

Unofficial Collaborator (IM); Assignment 203

Unofficial Collaborator (IM); Honesty 204

Unofficial Collaborator (IM); Prelude 204

Unofficial Collaborator (IM); Recruitment 205

Unofficial Collaborator (IM); Reparation and Reinsurance Motives 207

Unofficial Collaborator (IM); Stocktaking 207

Version 208

Warning Levels 209

Warning Signal 209

Who-Knows-Who Scheme (WKW) 210

Work on the Enemy 210

Young Cadres 211

Youth; Analysis of Movements and Concentrations 211

Youth; Operational Diversion 211

Youth; Operationally Interesting Grouping 212

Zionist Organizations 212

Abduction

A form of terror crime or general criminal offense. It involves forcibly taking people against their will using specific means and methods (violence, threats, deception, drugs, intoxicants, etc.) from their original location to other places, states, or areas. Terrorist abductions are characterized by:

- Planned and targeted selection of persons to be abducted.
- Threats to kill, mistreat, or harm the health of the abducted persons to exert extortionate pressure on state organs.
- Making specific demands to achieve broader terrorist goals.
- Efforts by the perpetrators to remain undetected and avoid direct confrontation with security organs.

Abductions can later escalate into → hostage-taking. Abductions can be associated with terror crimes under §§ 101, 102 StGB or crimes of anti-state human trafficking under § 105 StGB. If the conditions for a state crime are not met, it may involve a crime of human trafficking (§ 132 StGB) or the abduction of children or adolescents (§ 144 StGB).

See also aircraft hijacking.

Abduction of Persons

Transporting people against their will using specific means and methods (e.g., violence, threats, deception) from their original location to other places, states, or areas.

The abduction of DDR citizens abroad is a commission of anti-state human trafficking according to § 105 StGB. If the prerequisites for a state crime are not met, § 132 StGB - human trafficking - is to be considered for the mentioned actions.

see also: Kidnapping

Ability to Testify

Suitability of a person to make truthful and relevant statements due to their objective, real relationships to a particular fact. The quality and extent of the ability to testify are determined by the objectively accessible information to a person and the individual characteristics, abilities, and performances relevant for their perception and reproduction, particularly in perceiving, retaining, assessing, and evaluating, recognizing and reproducing, as well as by language comprehension and expressive ability, knowledge, and life experiences. For assessing the ability to testify, special attention must be paid to the promoting and inhibiting effects that current motives and emotions have both in capturing and reproducing the relevant information. The consideration of the ability to testify is important both in investigative work and in unofficial work. It should be taken into account that incomplete, misleading, false statements can result not only from deceptive intentions but also from a lack of ability to testify. The ability to testify of children and mentally ill persons always requires special examination, which may include psychological or specialist medical evaluation if necessary.

Ability, operative

Relatively consolidated, complex personality trait of operative forces that enables them to successfully and consistently perform tasks of a certain type of operational activities.

Operative abilities always interact with other personality traits (e.g., knowledge, skills, habits, attitudes, convictions, etc.) when dealing with specific activity requirements. They are essential performance prerequisites, expressed, for example, in the speed and ease of acquiring and performing an operational activity, the breadth of transferring to similar operational activities, and the quality or originality of operational work results.

Abilities develop and consolidate through the repeated practice of operational activities under the same or similar conditions based on previously acquired elementary abilities (e.g., perception, memory, thinking abilities), general abilities (e.g., understanding people, learning ability, assessment ability), acquired knowledge and experience, and other characteristics.

Essential abilities of operative forces include, for example:

- Ability to accurately identify the plans and intentions of the enemy and their attack directions,
- Ability to clearly and objectively recognize the means and methods of the enemy,
- Ability to actively and offensively work on suspicious and hostile individuals,
- Ability to always behave according to the rules of conspiracy, be vigilant, and ensure secrecy, etc.

Act of Treason

The commission of crimes representing crimes against the DDR or offenses and crimes of general criminality. It is characterized by the perpetrator revealing → state and official secrets under violation of an imposed duty to maintain confidentiality or (and) by abusing a position of trust.

A specific form of the act of treason can consist of military personnel and members of protection and security organs defecting to the enemy and delivering state and official secrets to them. Deviating from these characteristics of the act of treason, § 96 StGB (high treason) describes special acts of treason.

Criminal law provisions to combat acts of treason are §§ 96, 97-100, 172, 202, 245, 246, 272 StGB.

see also: Traitor

Action, Operationally Significant

A conscious, goal-oriented activity that, through its content, course, and result, affects the security interests of the DDR state and thus falls under the responsibility of the MfS. It can occur once and in isolation or as part of a complex activity.

For the MfS, both actions requiring operative handling and those that can be used in political-operative work are of interest.

The investigation and assessment of the motives and goals of an action lead to its precise security-political characterization and enable the initiation of differentiated political-operative measures.

Action, Operative

As part of political-operative activity, it is a conscious, goal-oriented activity of the MfS operative forces. The course and result depend on the internal and external conditions of the actor. The nature of the task, guidance, control, and evaluation of the action result can influence the internal regulation of the action and avoid errors. A purposeful sequence of the action phases (e.g., motivation and goal formation, consideration and decision preparation, decision, practical execution) is to be sought.

Agent Conservation

Temporary cessation of an agent's activities on the instructions of secret service employees, especially for security reasons, due to suspicion or acute justified possibilities of exposure or processing by socialist security organs. During agent conservation, there is usually no connection between the secret service and the agent.

The instructions and behavior guidelines established between them depending on the situation come into effect (→ sign of life). The agent usually destroys all documents and technical aids on instructions or stores them elsewhere (→ storage). At a suitable time, the further use of the conserved agent takes place. Secret services also recruit agents for specific subversive tasks to use them after a certain period of conservation when needed.

Agent Provocateur

An employee recruited by secret services, who is used domestically to infiltrate progressive parties, organizations, and associations, and is tasked with carrying out political provocations and other occasions, as well as with subversive measures.

Agent Radio Operator

An agent recruited by a secret service who transmits the information he has developed or collected himself, or received from other agents, to the headquarters via radio and usually receives instructions in the same way.

Agent Shutdown

Termination of the connection between secret services and their agents. Reasons for agent shutdown can include: exposure, proven lack of prospects, suspicion of operational processing by socialist security organs, factors that justify the "dishonesty" of the agents, subjective factors such as age, and other reasons.

Agent shutdown can, depending on the reasons, be associated with financial payments to the agents or their exfiltration to the territory of the clients.

Agent Smuggling

The conspiratorial transfer of secret service agents out of or into the territory of another state. Agent smuggling is carried out through the misuse of legal possibilities for crossing state borders by land, air, and waterways, as well as by using other means of crossing state borders (e.g., crossing the "green borders," using tunnels, etc.).

Agent Training

The process of political-ideological influence and professional qualification of agents to increase the effectiveness of their hostile activities by full-time employees or agents of the secret services. The scope, content, and form of agent training depend on the respective client, the specific mission direction of the agents and their importance to the client, the differentiated objectives of the training measures, the conditions under which agents operate hostilely and are to be trained, as well as the corresponding subjective prerequisites of the agent.

Agent-Handling Office

A conspiratorially covered facility of imperialist intelligence services that directly seeks, recruits, and deploys agents. These offices of imperialist intelligence services are often covered as civilian or military authorities, variable in structure and number of employees, and can change location and cover.

See also covert facility, intelligence; cover company.

Aircraft hijacking

The unlawful seizure of a civilian aircraft in flight by passengers or other occupants through violence or threat of violence, aiming to reach a state or area not intended in the flight plan or to extort demands from state authorities.

Aircraft hijacking is a form of terrorist crime (→ Terror). Aircraft hijacking significantly endangers people's lives and health and the safety of air traffic. Under certain conditions, they can affect the international relations of the DDR.

Aircraft hijacking is punishable under the law on criminal liability for hijacking aircraft from 12. 7. 1973, GBl. I Nr. 33, p. 337, as a crime. Furthermore, aircraft hijacking usually reaches the quality of → state crime.

Aircraft hijackers are fundamentally hostile forces acting based on consolidated anti-state attitudes, motives, and goals, possessing high risk-taking willingness and readiness to use brutal and dangerous means and methods, such as firearms and explosives. In individual cases, aircraft hijacking as part of serious common criminal offenses or actions of mentally disturbed individuals cannot be ruled out.

Alternative Legend

Prepared variant of a → Legend that is used when unexpected complications, difficulties, or changed conditions arise in the resolution of politically-operative tasks, and corresponding operationally appropriate reactions/behavior of the operational forces are necessary.

Analysis of Person Movements

A method for determining and verifying the movement patterns of persons and vehicles associated with a politically-operative significant → incident or event. The analysis of person movements aims to:

- Identify all individuals who were present or moved in a specific area at a particular time,
- Record and evaluate all observations, clues, etc., from this group of individuals that may be related to the incident or event under investigation,
- Identify and operatively and evidentially evaluate contradictions in the statements of individual persons.

For a thorough and precise analysis of person movements, it is particularly necessary to:

- Precisely determine the time and location of the incident or event under investigation,
- Accurately determine the probable path of the perpetrator, their method of operation, and the time required to carry out the act,

- Thoroughly prepare and instruct all employees involved in questioning the identified group of persons,
- Conscientiously register and carefully verify all gathered clues, contradictions, etc.

A suitable method for the quantitative analysis of movement patterns is working with the → time-distance diagram.

Analytical Work

The necessary mental performance in politically-operative work and management activities for the correct reflection and politically-operative and legal assessment of operationally significant facts, persons, interrelations, etc., for deriving justified conclusions and decisions, and for the purposeful presentation of the findings obtained in this way. The content of Analytical Work is determined by the task of politically-operative work or management activity that it must help to solve. The basis of Analytical Work is the security policy-relevant findings underlying all operational work processes, especially from documents of the party and state leadership, official regulations and instructions, as well as from previous assessments of operationally significant facts, persons, interrelations, etc.

In the process of Analytical Work, individual or combined information, operational materials, and other documents are mentally dissected into their components, ordered, compared, and related, condensed, and mentally or purposefully summarized at a qualitatively higher level. The general goal of Analytical Work is to gain necessary insights for solving politically-operative work tasks, justify necessary decisions in politically-operative work, and prepare operationally significant information and insights for purposeful informing and storage. Analytical Work to solve tasks of politically-operative work and management activities must be performed by every manager and employee. It is an inseparable part of politically-operative work.

Analytical Work; Methods

Requirements, regulations, or rules that are applied as guidelines for forming true statements, conclusions, or generalizations in Analytical Work. The method to be applied is determined by the goal and subject of Analytical Work as well as the usable initial information. The most essential methods of Analytical Work are:

- the method for mentally developing a preliminary picture as a comparison object,
- the method of comparison to recognize analogies,
- the method of difference,
- the method of agreement,
- the method of accompanying change,
- the method of gaining insights through the enumeration of essential features. Practically widespread analysis methods are the target-actual comparison, the time comparison, and the object comparison.

Annual Plan of Political-Operative Work

A binding official document for the focused organization and execution of political-operative work and its management over a calendar year. The annual plan contains binding determinations of essential goals, tasks, and measures to ensure security in the area of responsibility, particularly to secure political-operative key areas and to address political-operative focal points. It specifies the necessary deployment and further development of operational forces and means, as well as the essential tasks and measures of leadership activity and their further improvement.

Annual plans are developed by all leaders, mid-level management cadres, and employees. In small departments and working groups, the employees' tasks can be fully included in the plan of the department or group leader. By the leader's decision, individual employees may have → security concepts or other planning documents replace the annual plan. With the confirmation by the superior leader, the annual plan becomes an instruction.

The foundations for drafting the annual plan are the resolutions and documents of the party and state leadership, official regulations and instructions, → plan directives, → plan orientations, the assessment of the → political-operative situation, and applicable → long-term concepts for the area of responsibility.

Anti-Constitutional Conspiracy

An assembly of persons under § 107 StGB whose actions aim at hostile activities against the constitutional foundations. Anti-constitutional conspiracies are particularly characterized by:

- The joint development of programs, concepts, platforms, etc., proclaiming their hostile objectives;
- An independently developed organizational and communication relationship;
- The use of conspiratorial, intelligence means and methods;
- Establishing communication relationships with other internal and external hostile forces;
- The misuse of legal opportunities for hostile objectives.

Anti-constitutional conspiracies can appear in conjunction with other state crimes and general criminal offenses. They pose a high social danger, requiring attention to the individual criminal responsibility of members of anti-constitutional conspiracies.

Antisocial Behavior

Occurs when a person behaves contrary to social norms in a particular situation.

Antisocial behavior can occur in all areas of social life. It ranges from the violation of moral norms to all kinds of legal violations, including criminal offenses.

For political-operational activities, it is important to determine why a person decided to engage in the specific antisocial behavior and how their behavior can be explained. Furthermore, it is necessary to examine and assess how such persons can be used by the enemy for their subversive activities, what contradictions underlie the behavior, to contribute to the clarification of "Who is who?".

The concrete content of the behavior and the personality determine the extent to which state and social reactions are carried out by which organs and organizations.

Behavior must be distinguished from the term → antisociality as a characteristic of a criminal act.

Anti-State Activity

The entirety of actions carried out by hostile forces/persons, organizations, intelligence services, institutions, and other groups of persons directed against the constitutional foundations of the socialist social and state order. Anti-state activity manifests itself in crimes against the sovereignty of the DDR, peace, humanity, and human rights, as well as in crimes against the DDR described in Chapters I and II of the Special Part of the StGB.

Archiving

The process of transferring completed registered cases and files and other operationally significant documents to the operational unit responsible for centralized record-keeping and archiving within the MfS. Archiving serves to preserve and securely store operationally significant documents and make them available for information retrieval and renewed operational use by authorized members of the MfS or operational units. Archiving includes the decision of the head of the case or file-keeping operational unit on archiving, the preparation of operationally significant documents for transfer to the archive, the assignment of a special registration number (archive signature) by the record-keeping operational unit, and the inclusion in the archive inventory.

Arrest, preliminary

A temporary restriction of personal freedom, a coercive measure in criminal procedure, through which a person suspected of a crime is immediately apprehended and held for a limited time without a previously obtained arrest warrant, if the legal conditions are met.

The StPO distinguishes the arrest authority for anyone if a person is caught in the act or pursued and suspected of flight or if their identity cannot be immediately established (§ 125 Abs. 1 StPO), and the arrest authority for the prosecutor and investigation organ if the conditions of an arrest warrant are met and there is imminent danger (§ 125 Abs. 2 StPO).

Preliminary arrest has particular significance in the political-operative work of the MfS as a closing variant of an → Operative process. The following requirements must be observed:

1. Preliminary arrest according to § 125 Abs. 1 StPO (arrest in the act) must be prepared and conducted in such a way that:
    - An unequivocal official evidence situation arises in connection with the arrest situation, justifying the suspicion of a crime,
    - Objective documentation of the evidence situation is ensured,
    - If necessary, unofficial forces and conspiratorial means and methods are distracted,
    - The element of surprise can be used to induce a quick willingness to testify.

The arrest according to § 125 Abs. 1 StPO can be carried out by all employees of the MfS. As a closing variant of an Operative process, it must, however, be coordinated and prepared with the responsible investigation department according to guideline 1/76. If it occurs unexpectedly without prior political-operative information, the investigation department must be informed immediately.

2. The arrest authority of the MfS investigation organs according to § 125 Abs. 2 StPO is to be used mainly when the criminally relevant actions of the suspect in the Operative process have been clarified to the extent that the conditions of an arrest warrant and imminent danger are affirmed, but obtaining the arrest warrant beforehand must be omitted, especially for reasons of conspiracy. If such a closing variant of an Operative process is proposed, the responsible investigation department must be consulted at the latest before the conclusion of the Operative process. Preliminary arrest according to § 125 Abs. 2 StPO is carried out by employees of the investigation department or by employees of other political-operative service units if expressly authorized by the head of the investigation organ.

Preliminary arrest ends with the issuance of an arrest warrant or the release of the arrested person. The deadlines mentioned in § 126 Abs. 4 and 5 StPO must be observed.

Asociality

A social behavior, including the underlying asocial attitudes and the resulting social phenomena, through which individual persons or groups of persons (asocials) temporarily or permanently position themselves in extreme opposition to parts or the entire framework of moral and legal norms of social life in the socialist society. Asociality is associated with the deformation of the personal lifestyle and the social bonds of the respective persons. Asociality is an alien phenomenon to socialism. It is caused by remnants of the capitalist society still existing within the DDR as well as current influences from the imperialist ruling system. Of particular importance are the effects of political-ideological diversion and the mass dissemination of bourgeois subculture and decadent lifestyle in the FRG and West Berlin on politically and morally unstable persons in the DDR.

Asociality affects fundamental social relationships, particularly the relationship between humans and work in socialism. Asociality, therefore, manifests itself primarily in the permanent rejection of regulated work and the consequent acquisition of livelihood in dishonest ways, such as speculation, prostitution, etc. Asocial behavior can have a corrosive effect on the further development of socialist consciousness and socially appropriate, socialist behaviors, be the cause or starting point for criminal offenses of general crime, especially against state order and against personality, and favor crimes against the socialist state and social order. Asociality reaches the quality of criminal offenses when asocial behavior endangers the social coexistence of citizens or public order — endangering public order through asocial behavior, § 249 StGB.

A criminal offense may also be present when children or adolescents are induced by adults to adopt an asocial lifestyle — inducing asocial lifestyle, § 145 StGB. Asociality with its negative impacts on socialist social relationships objectively serves the enemy. The enemy aims to inspire mainly young people and young adults of the DDR with asocial behaviors through demagogic slogans, especially to resist state and public order, but also to attack the socialist state and social order of the DDR. The application of legally justified state measures against persons and groups with asocial behaviors (e.g., according to the regulation on the tasks of local councils and enterprises in the education of criminally endangered citizens from 19.12.1974, GBl. I Nr. 6 S. 130) is particularly defamed by imperialist mass media as alleged violations of human rights.

Assassination

A form of high treason or terrorist crimes. Assassinations are direct hostile attacks against the life and health of persons. If assassinations are directed against leading representatives of the DDR or allied states, the presence of a high treason enterprise is given according to § 96 StGB (possibly in connection with § 108 StGB).

Target persons are usually those whose killing the perpetrators hope will cause a particularly high degree of damage to the DDR, destabilize social conditions, create fear and terror among the population, etc. The means used include firearms, cutting, stabbing, and other weapons, explosives, poisons, acids, etc., which can also kill, injure, or endanger uninvolved persons and destroy or damage material assets.

See also Attack.

Assessment of the Political-Operational Situation

The mental process of creating an objective picture of the political-operational situation in which the political-operational work in the area of responsibility is to be led and carried out. This mental process is the unity of analysis and political-operational evaluation of the factors of the political-operational situation from the perspective of the political-operational task to ensure the protection of social development and state security in the area of responsibility. Generally, the picture of the political-operational situation obtained as a result of this mental process is also referred to as the assessment of the situation.

The assessment must always be task-oriented as an inseparable part of political-operational work to create the necessary foundations for the realization of operational processes and leadership activities. It is realized in a multifaceted process of analytical work that must permeate the political-operational thinking of every leader and employee.

This process of continuous updating, concretization, and perfection of the assessment of the situation extends from the assessment of daily information inflow in the area of responsibility to the preparation of specific assessments and decisions on operational cases, operational occurrences, operationally significant persons, etc., the creation of operational analyses to assess the situation in political-operational focal areas or specific problems, up to the assessment of the situation in the overall area of responsibility.

Asylum Request

The application of a foreigner to the responsible state organs of the DDR to grant him protection from persecution by granting permission to stay in the DDR. The DDR grants asylum to foreigners who are persecuted for their political, scientific, or cultural activities in defense of peace, democracy, the interests of the working people, or for their participation in the social and national liberation struggle. Asylum can also be granted for other political reasons. The asylum seeker is protected from persecution, expulsion, and extradition by asylum (Article 23, Constitution of the DDR). Asylum is a right granted by states to asylum seekers.

There is no legal right to asylum, and states are not obligated to grant asylum. Asylum seekers receive the necessary permits for their stay in the DDR according to the Foreigners Ordinance of June 28, 1979.

In the DDR, the right to asylum, which is bound to strict, confidential regulations, is administered by the central state organs. On their behalf, the protection and security organs must conduct verification actions before and after the granting of asylum to prevent enemy misuse, exclude it as far as possible, or detect it in time. If misuse is found, asylum can be revoked. It can also be revoked if it is subsequently determined that the asylum seeker provided false information or if reasons emerge that, if known before the granting of asylum, would have led to the rejection of the asylum request.

Attacks Against the Ministry for State Security (MfS)

A significant component of the broader system of subversive and other hostile activities of imperialism against real socialism. The MfS, as a crucial instrument of the dictatorship of the proletariat, plays a key role in combating particularly subversive efforts to achieve counter-revolutionary goals and intentions of imperialism. Consequently, the MfS has become a primary target for the enemy, especially for the core of its subversive organs, the imperialist intelligence services. The main goal of increasingly coordinated, division-of-labor attacks against the MfS, orchestrated chiefly by intelligence services and centrally coordinated by the highest imperialist leadership bodies, is to undermine the political-operational effectiveness, combat readiness, and reliability of the MfS in ensuring the state security of the DDR. The aim is to erode the trust of the party in the MfS, discredit it in the eyes of the public, and ultimately, if possible, neutralize it.

The primary directions of these attacks by the main enemy of the MfS, the imperialist intelligence services, have been identified as:

- The reconnaissance and targeting of current and former MfS employees, their families, and acquaintances, as well as potential MfS personnel, with the intention of carrying out recruitment through softening and undermining, or creating and utilizing compromising material to infiltrate the MfS apparatus or obtain secret information about security organs through intelligence collection,

- The exploration of MfS plans and intentions, its structure, measures, methods, and means of clarifying and countering all hostile attacks, especially those involving unofficial forces in the operations area and in the DDR, the internal cooperation between MfS structural units, and its collaboration with allied brother organizations, particularly the Soviet Chekists, to identify opportunities for subversive attacks,

- The reconnaissance and partial surveillance of official and unofficial objects, as well as MfS residential areas, to identify and target individuals as MfS members or unofficial collaborators and create prerequisites for other actions, including potentially terrorist actions, as well as exploring the official cooperation of the MfS with other security forces and state and social institutions in the DDR, to gain attack points.

In addition to the existence and activities of "specialists" and specially designated structural units, the intelligence services increasingly utilize their entire apparatus and all → agents, depending on available opportunities, for attacks against the MfS and other socialist security organs. The focus is on → espionage through direct reconnaissance and → intelligence collection, to create so-called basic material as a prerequisite for further targeted actions against the MfS. On this basis, the enemy particularly aims to paralyze, mislead, disinform, and unsettle the MfS, especially to induce political and other erroneous decisions by the party and government through false information activities of our organ. This underscores the high societal danger of attacks, particularly by the imperialist intelligence services, against the MfS and the objective necessity of ensuring the internal security of the MfS at all times.

Attitude

A personality trait acquired in dealing with the environment, which as an object-related inner readiness to act and react, relatively consistently directs experience and behavior. Attitudes play an important role in all operational and operationally interesting actions because they facilitate personal decisions, allow appropriate orientation in action situations from the perspective of the actor, and internally condition adherence to certain norms and rules, overall acting as motivation.

Attitudes towards the world and society, other people and collectives, work, and oneself can develop in a versatile and differentiated manner in individuals. Precise knowledge of attitudes allows highly probable predictions of future behavior. With strong consolidation and generalization, attitudes can take on the quality of convictions. These are usually of ideological and scientific content and have a central significance in a person's thinking and way of life. As socialist, religious, humanistic, or even anti-communist convictions, they can significantly determine overall behavior.

Attitude Analysis

Procedure for assessing the attitudes and convictions of individuals in political-operative work. The attitude analysis is required to solve tasks in cadre work (e.g., assessing candidates for service in the MfS, MfS employees, etc.). It is also part of the evaluation of → operationally significant persons in operational processes, such as IM work, processing of operational procedures, security checks, etc. Since attitudes and convictions are not directly observable, they must be inferred indirectly from actions, statements, and behaviors. This requires a conscious, methodical approach in the following steps:

- Determining the goals of the attitude analysis (which attitudes and convictions should be identified?).
- Gathering information about actions, statements, and behaviors through material analysis, behavior observation, and conversation.
- Deriving the general and essential behavior of the person regarding the interesting attitude objects (e.g., ideology, activity, persons, etc.).
- Drawing conclusions about the attitudes and convictions according to the goals of the attitude analysis.

The identified attitudes must be described and assessed differentiatedly according to content, degree of expression, stability, structure, and action effectiveness, as well as the course and conditions of their development and possibilities for change.

Attitude Formation

Procedure for developing or changing attitudes and convictions of individuals in political-operative work. It is part of the education of operational forces (e.g., developing positive attitudes of operational employees towards unofficial work, conveying the enemy image to informal forces, etc.). Attitude formation is also required for the long-term influence of → operationally significant persons to achieve political and operational goals. Attitudes and convictions are formed in political-operative work under specific educational conditions. The great diversity and often complicated interplay of external factors affecting a person and their specific internal conditions must be considered. The necessary stability of attitudes and convictions is more likely to be achieved if the educational impulses are consciously, repeatedly, and personally set. Additionally, the random influence of current factors must be considered positively and negatively.

Operational experiences and scientific findings suggest applying the following basic principles of conviction and attitude formation:

- Role model effect (conscious learning process where exemplary behaviors of others are adopted).
- Instruction (form of influence where it is communicated which attitude is required or rejected).
- Guidance (setting a task where specific attitudes arise inevitably without discussing it).
- Motivation (approach where repeated occurrences of current motives, caused by continuous setting of inner contradictions, solidify motives into relatively stable attitudes).
- Sanctioning (conscious evaluation of behavior to confirm or weaken motives, attitudes, and convictions).
- Imitation (unconscious adoption of behaviors).

In their application, these basic principles do not stand alongside other possibilities of educational influence but form their principal psychological content.

Attitudes towards the MfS

These express the relationship a person has or develops with the MfS through their behavior. In the various forms of cooperation with the MfS, the diverse and different attitudes of the persons involved must be considered and utilized. They are developed and consolidated through attitude formation, especially by:

- The various contacts with the MfS, where citizens gain insights, experiences, and convictions about working with the MfS (public relations work, official and unofficial cooperation).
- The individual impact of the MfS's successes in the fight against the enemy.
- The consistent adherence to socialist legality.
- The exemplary personal behavior of each employee.

The greater the effectiveness of these factors, the less the enemy can generate negative, rejecting attitudes through → manipulation of consciousness. Especially with IM who agreed to cooperate without positive political convictions, it is possible and necessary to neutralize existing negative attitudes, including anti-socialist attitudes, systematically and achieve operational and educational successes in cooperation.

Authorization System

The entirety of the state procedure for granting permits, approvals, licenses, consents, and authorizations to legal entities (individuals, collectives, enterprises, institutions, and social organizations) for performing certain activities and exercising certain rights. The authorization system is regulated by legal provisions and managed by the competent state organs of the DDR. It serves to protect the interests of the socialist social and state order and its citizens, as well as to ensure order and security. Of operational relevance are particularly the permits issued by the DVP, central state organs, and local councils. The DVP is responsible, among other things, for:

- Manufacturing, distributing, storing, transporting, possessing, and using explosives,
- Manufacturing, handling, distributing, importing, exporting, and transiting, storing, acquiring, possessing, and using firearms and ammunition,
- Manufacturing, obtaining, processing, storing, using, acquiring, possessing, and dispensing Class 1 poisons,
- Operating a motor vehicle on public roads,
- Conducting events that require approval,
- Entering and exiting the DDR's state border,
- Entering and staying in border areas,
- Shortening or lifting curfew hours.

Central state organs and local councils are responsible, within the scope of legally defined competencies, for authorization regarding:

- The founding and activities of associations,
- Conducting collections and lotteries,
- Performing dance and entertainment music and authorizing discos,
- Establishing and using campgrounds, temporary shelters, and makeshift accommodations,
- Producing printed and duplicated materials,
- Engaging in trades and certain professions,
- Transactions involving real estate,
- Constructing and altering buildings.

All authorizations require the following fundamental conditions:

- State interest,

- Social need and personal interests,
- Personal reliability and qualification of the applicants.

The competent state organs may restrict, revoke, withdraw, declare invalid, or impose conditions on authorizations under certain circumstances as provided by the relevant legal provisions. The decisive conditions for this include:

- The legal prerequisites for granting or issuing the authorization are no longer met,
- The holder of the authorization violates the legal provisions concerning the tasks, duties, and rights associated with the granted authorization,
- The conditions imposed with the issuance of the authorization are violated,
- Authorizations are misused.

In the → political-operational cooperation of the MfS with the competent state organs, the political-operational interests to ensure state security, particularly in the application, examination, and decision-making process, as well as in monitoring compliance with legal provisions and imposed conditions, must be implemented in the area of authorization.

Behavior Disorder

Behavior of a person that is repeatedly or constantly inappropriate to the current situation to a lesser or greater extent due to pathological disturbances of mental activity, and therefore more or less noticeable. Pathological disturbances of mental activity arise because experienced or actual discrepancies between a person's behavioral and performance capabilities on one hand and the demands of the environment on the other hand lead to perceived or actual overstrain or understrain situations, as a result of which the respective person can get into conflicts that they can hardly or not at all resolve alone. These conflicts are processed inappropriately internally. Incorrect attitudes arise, which exacerbate the conflicts with the environment, can lead to psychological disturbances with disease value, and manifest as behavior disorders.

Impacts of behavior disorders are evident in the impairment of relationships with other people and the unsatisfactory coping with demands. They are accompanied by physical and psychological complaints. As a result, various performance impairments can occur. Physical and psychological general complaints can include, for example, headaches, blushing, and sweating, mood swings, fatigue, concentration difficulties, jumpiness, and as specific physical complaints without organ damage can include, for example, disorders of stomach, intestinal, heart, circulatory, respiratory, and gland functions.

In interpersonal relationships, difficulties manifest, for example, in inhibition towards other people, inhibitions towards people of the opposite sex, feelings of inferiority, but also in exaggerated need for recognition, bragging, irritability, aggressiveness, sexual perversions, etc.

The operational significance of behavior disorders lies in:

- the inability or restriction to fulfill operational, professional, and social tasks,
- the increase in security risk, endangerment of conspiracy, secrecy, and vigilance associated with their occurrence,
- the possibility that actions and behaviors of people that objectively violate social norms or criminal statutes can subjectively, without limitation of criminal responsibility according to §§ 15, 16 StGB, be present.

When identifying behavior disorders, the causes must be examined with the involvement of specialists (doctors, psychologists, expert IM) and suitable differentiated measures must be determined according to the given necessities and possibilities.

Border Area

A defined and marked strip of land along the state border established on a state basis, with depth determined by domestic regulations and where special legal provisions apply to ensure order and security.

The establishment of the border area along the DDR state border with the BRD and West Berlin, including the sea border, was based on the Ordinance for the Protection of the DDR State Border. Along the DDR state border with the BRD, the border area consists of the protection strip and the restricted zone. Along the DDR state border with West Berlin, the border area consists of a protection strip. Along the DDR coast, the border area consists of the protection strip (from Pötenitzer Wiek to Steinbeck, Kreis Grevesmühlen) and the border zone, including the internal sea waters.

The restricted zone is the strip of land, with depth defined by the rear boundary of the protection strip and the course of the border area (about 3-5 km). The border zone is the strip of land along the DDR coast, with depth defined by the coastline's baseline and a line about 5 km deep running parallel to the baseline (including the islands of Poel, Rügen, Hiddensee, and Usedom, as well as the peninsulas of Darß and Wustrow).

The protection strip is an area with depth defined by the immediate course of the state border and the course of the restricted zone (depending on territorial conditions, about 50-500 m deep). It includes the action area of the DDR border troops as a military restricted area.

Border Provocation

Hostile acts that violate the sovereignty and territorial integrity of the DDR, directed against border security forces and installations, as well as against the population in the DDR border areas, to provoke the DDR state organs, especially the border security forces, into behaviors beneficial to the enemy and harmful to the DDR.

Goals of border provocations can include:

- Preparing, triggering, or justifying acts of aggression and other international conflicts,
- Creating tensions and insecurity at the state border and in the border area,
- Reconnoitering and disrupting the DDR border security system,
- Testing the DDR organs' countermeasures,
- Enabling other hostile acts like state-hostile human trafficking or infiltrating subversive forces,
- Discrediting the DDR internationally, etc.

Border provocations are part of the aggressive policies of imperialism and are committed by hostile forces (civilian, military personnel, border security forces, etc.) from imperialist countries and by DDR citizens acting in the enemy's interest or under their orders. Border provocations endanger peace and international relations and are often acts against international law.

Given the goals mentioned above, border provocations can manifest as:

- Violent attacks against border security forces and the population in border areas (threatening or using weapons, explosives, other means of violence),
- Attacks against border security installations, markings, and signage of the state border,
- Crossing, overflying, or swimming across the state border by individuals, groups, military formations, aircraft, ships, etc.,
- Acts of state-hostile agitation (calls for desertion, agitation events, etc.).

Border Security Forces

Members of protection and security organs and individuals acting on their behalf, tasked with implementing border security measures, particularly in the border area, based on existing legal regulations. Border security forces include:

- Members of the DDR border troops,
- Members of the People's Navy of the NVA (Coastal Border Brigade),
- Members of the Ministry of the Interior,
- Employees of the Ministry for State Security, including IM,
- Employees of the DDR Customs Administration,
- Volunteer helpers of the DVP and DDR border troops.

Border Violation

An illegal act by one or more persons, usually involving unauthorized crossing of the state border. Objectives of border violations can include:

- Entering or leaving DDR territory,
- Damaging or destroying border security installations,
- Hindering the activities of border security forces, etc.

In some cases, a border violation may occur without the violator having the stated objectives (e.g., malfunction of navigation equipment in ships and aircraft).

Border violations are often associated with hostile activities, such as state-hostile human trafficking, terrorist crimes, espionage, etc., as well as certain general criminal activities (e.g., illegal border crossing, customs and currency offenses). They can escalate into serious international conflicts (e.g., border provocations, reasons for starting acts of aggression).

Border violation differs from → border provocation by its different objective and generally lesser objective severity, although the external appearance may be similar.

Breach of Duty

An action that objectively contradicts social, legal, or moral duties imposed on a legal subject by society, the state, custom, or tradition. Breach of duty involves a specific violation of the social requirements raised by socialist society for socially appropriate and responsible behavior of the individual. Breach of duty can lead to harmful consequences for society, the state, collectives, communities, or individual citizens. Breach of duty is committed culpably, either intentionally or negligently. Depending on the social relations protected by socialist society, the content and extent of breach of duty establish criminal, administrative, especially regulatory, economic, labor, civil, disciplinary, social, or moral responsibility. The state's or society's reaction (sanction) following breach of duty has an educational character and is primarily directed at making the legal subjects accountable for their breach of duty before socialist society and its citizens through restitution and proof, as well as overcoming the damage or danger caused by breach of duty or restoring the previous state. Breach of duty deserves constant attention in political-operative work. Visible minor or simple breaches of duty can contain clues for serious breaches of duty or develop into such if ignored. A specific definition for criminal law is provided in § 9 StGB.

Bringing in

A measure that temporarily restricts personal freedom, whereby a person is taken from their current location to a state office by authorized security personnel of the DDR based on applicable legal provisions. In the political-operative work of the MfS, a bringing in is carried out mainly to question the brought-in person in connection with the clarification of politically operative and, if necessary, criminally relevant actions or when other politically operative objectives are legally justified.

The execution of a bringing in is possible based on different legal provisions:

1. Bringing in as a criminal procedural measure according to § 95 Abs. 2 StPO is only permissible against a suspect if it is indispensable for questioning. Only employees of the MfS's investigative organs or employees of other politically operative units with explicit authorization from the head of the investigative organ are entitled to perform such a bringing in (§ 95 Abs. 1 StPO).

Bringing in as → police authority according to § 12 Abs. 2 VPG is permissible if the person's identity cannot be clearly established on the spot or if it is essential for clarifying a situation that significantly endangers public order and safety. The authority can be exercised by any MfS employee according to § 20 Abs. 2 VPG.

2. Authorities of other state organs that arise from other legal provisions (e.g., customs law, border regulations, reporting regulations, conscription law, regulation on the tasks of local councils and enterprises in educating criminally endangered citizens) can be used in cooperation with these organs for politically operative purposes.

Cadre Reserve

Members of the MfS who have been prepared and tested for deployment in leadership positions according to the nomenclature and are deployable as needed. The cadre reserve is to be created according to the actual need for filling leadership positions, for an foreseeable period. Members of the cadre reserve must distinguish themselves by:

- Party loyalty, commitment, and determination as well as moral maturity,
- High Marxist-Leninist, political-operative, and professional knowledge, extensive experience in political work, and abilities to solve political-operative tasks,
- Qualification for the intended position or prerequisites for acquiring it, task-related military-chekist or staff work knowledge,
- Leadership qualities for managing collectives and employees, physical and psychological resilience.

Members of the cadre reserve are to be developed primarily through the work process and through attending schools and courses. The corresponding determinations in cadre programs and plans are to be individually specified and systematically implemented.

Case Processing

An operational process for clarifying the suspicion of anti-state activity or operationally significant crimes of general criminality, for whose processing the MfS is responsible according to official regulations and instructions, in → operational processes. The subject of case processing is planned, prepared, attempted, or already carried out actions by known or unknown individuals - including the intentions, goals, and motives underlying these actions - from which the suspicion arises, as well as those characteristics of the perpetrator's personality that are significant according to the grounds of suspicion.

Case processing is:

- The most specific, direct, offensive fight against the conspiratorial enemy,
- Very closely linked to the implementation of fundamental questions of the strategy and tactics of the party and state leadership,

- The complex and carefully coordinated use of all operational forces, means, and methods - with the primacy of the IM,
- The unity of prevention, detection, prevention, and processing.

The politically operative objectives of case processing are:

- To provide the necessary evidence to prove the urgent suspicion through an offensive, concentrated, and fact-related processing - considering all exculpatory and incriminating circumstances,
- To timely restrict or prevent the recognized or expected socially harmful effects of anti-state activities or other crimes throughout the processing,
- To identify, prove, and largely restrict or eliminate the conditions and circumstances causing or favoring anti-state activities or other crimes during processing,
- To comprehensively and continuously clarify the plans, intentions, and measures of imperialist intelligence services and other hostile centers, organizations, and forces and to timely and effectively prevent their realization through appropriate politically operative measures.

The success-determining factors of case processing are primarily: appropriate leadership; offensive approach (especially in using IM through operational → legends and combinations); concentration of operational forces and means on achieving the goals of processing the operational process; conspiracy and confidentiality; adherence to and enforcement of socialist legality; ensuring the necessary cooperation and operational → coordination.

Centers of Political-Ideological Subversion

Special organs and facilities of imperialist states that play a significant role in planning, directing, and shaping political-ideological subversion, selecting appropriate means and methods, and organizing and carrying out political-ideological attacks. From a political-operative perspective, the centers are divided into leading, research, and executing organs based on their main functions. Leading organs, such as the Federal Ministry for Intra-German Relations, certain NATO committees, and system-supporting parties, primarily have tasks of central planning, directing, and coordinating political-ideological subversion. Research organs, such as the organs of so-called East and DDR research in the BRD, develop proposals for the content and methodical design of political-ideological attacks using scientific methods, such as concepts and guidelines. They also analyze the effectiveness of political-ideological subversion in socialist countries, among other things. Executing organs, such as the mass media and certain enemy organizations, directly carry out political-ideological subversion. The centers are closely connected with the imperialist intelligence services to achieve high effectiveness of ideological attacks through coordinated and divided actions.

Central Enemy Object Case (ZFOV)

Compilation of all essential political-operative findings on the enemy activities of specifically defined hostile entities and forces, such as imperialist intelligence services, criminal human trafficking gangs, and other enemy organizations that act against significant societal areas or developmental processes in the DDR.

The ZFOV ensures the concentrated consolidation, systematic documentation, and assessment of politically operative significant information and evidence. ZFOVs are managed by central operative units in the MfS to enforce a unified orientation and effective coordination of the politically operative work of all units involved in combating the hostile entities and forces. The work with ZFOV aims to achieve:

- Continuous current overview of the plans, intentions, and activities directed against the DDR and other socialist states by hostile entities, their attack directions, target objects, target

persons, means and methods, individuals working for or on behalf of hostile entities, and regime conditions, identifying backgrounds and contexts of enemy activities;
- Development of central orientations and concepts, especially for processing central operational cases and operational cases;
- Creation of prerequisites for an offensive, socially and politically effective fight against hostile entities;
- Quick, accurate classification, and operational assessment of individual information;
- Generalization of operational experiences in the fight against hostile entities and forces;
- Consolidation and summarization of information for the Party and state leadership.

ZFOVs are a specific form of evaluation processes.

Central Operational Case (ZOV)

→ Operational case, in which the centralized, fact-based operational processing of hostile entities and forces takes place. It encompasses the entire process of complex, coordinated, and harmonized operational processing aimed at a unified goal.

The subject of ZOV processing are the crimes, attacks, or impacts of hostile entities and forces directed against the DDR and other socialist states when they exhibit or are expected to exhibit high social danger and relate to the responsibilities of several operational units. The processing essentially focuses on the actions of individuals from which the suspicion of violating criminal laws of the StGB and other legal violations arises.

The operational processing of the individual, closely interrelated operational cases as parts (→ subcases) of the whole (ZOV) must be carried out independently by all operational units involved in the processing based on a processing concept under the leadership of a ZOV-leading unit. To achieve the ZOV processing goals, targeted operational processing must be organized and conducted in close, comradely collaboration between the ZOV-leading unit and the subcase-processing units.

Central Person Database (ZPDB)

A central electronic storage and retrieval system of the MfS for operationally significant information on persons, facts, characteristics, and clues to support politically operative work and its management.

The ZPDB enables the consolidation of information on a person, fact, clue, or characteristic and the rapid retrieval of stored information in any possible combination according to the established authorities, especially for the political-operative assessment of the situation, the investigation of operationally significant incidents, and the development and processing of operational cases.

Chain of Circumstantial Evidence

An important methodological element of the circumstantial evidence.

The chain of circumstantial evidence represents such a combination of information from indirect → evidence (→ indications) and established scientific findings that lead to → evidence facts. The prerequisites for this are that:

- the objective truth of each piece of information inherent in the individual indirect evidence is unequivocally proven,

the individual pieces of information are objectively related to each other and to the subject of → evidence presentation,

- a sufficient number of indirect evidence is available, allowing for the formation of a closed chain,
- the connection between individual pieces of information and established scientific findings is in accordance with logical laws,
- the chain thus formed is complete and free of contradictions,

- the findings obtained as a result exclude any other plausible explanation with certainty.

Chekist Personality

A socialist personality who, as a member of a socialist security organ, fights directly and under the leadership of the workers' party for the protection of socialism and the comprehensive and reliable security of the power of the working class against all subversive attacks by the class enemy. It is shaped and developed through active work for the construction and protection of socialist and communist society, especially in the process of conspiratorial chekist work, the uncompromising fight against the enemy, and the necessary chekist education and training.

A chekist personality is characterized primarily by such personality traits necessary for chekist work, such as:

- Absolute loyalty and deep connection to the working class and its Marxist-Leninist party,
- Unshakeable friendship with the Soviet Union and other socialist brother countries, attitudes and behaviors determined by socialist patriotism and internationalism,
- Willingness for continuous learning, especially in acquiring the Marxist-Leninist worldview and deepening the understanding of the party's policies,
- Determination, courage, politically wise chekist actions, willingness to sacrifice, and hatred in the fight against the enemy based on a clear enemy image,
- Willingness and ability to maintain secrecy and ensure the internal security of the state security organs,
- Creative initiative, high military discipline, open and honest demeanor, modesty, critical and self-critical behavior in and outside chekist activities,

- Willpower and consistency in maintaining and promoting physical and mental performance, meaningful use of leisure time.

These and similar personality traits must be developed and strengthened in the chekist work process and in the process of education.

Churches; Misuse of

A form of enemy activity aimed at inspiring, organizing, and conducting → political underground activity and creating internal anti-socialist opposition movements. The misuse of churches in the DDR is characterized by attempts by hostile entities and church institutions in the operational area, in cooperation with hostile-negative forces within and outside the churches, to expand or exceed the legally secured scope of action of churches in the DDR and to misuse the legal ecclesiastical means for anti-socialist goals. The enemy and hostile-negative forces particularly try to exploit the ideological positions of the churches, which are contrary to Marxism-Leninism, their close ties to churches in the BRD, West Berlin, and other capitalist states, their relative material independence, existing church structures, organizational forms, and material-technical possibilities, as well as the well-trained and ideologically influential church personnel to influence large sections of the population to achieve and conceal their anti-socialist activities. Actions that constitute misuse of churches in the DDR (misuse actions) mainly involve establishing connections and cooperating with hostile entities and forces as well as church institutions in the operational area, creating or adopting and disseminating anti-socialist concepts and platforms, seeking, collecting, and bringing together hostile-negative forces and misguided individuals, and preparing and conducting anti-socialist actions and measures.

These misuse actions are characterized by the following legal criteria:

1. They do not constitute solely religious activity within the meaning of the constitutional right to free exercise of religion.
2. They violate the principles and goals of the DDR's constitution.
3. They usually infringe specific legal obligations under other DDR legal regulations.
4. They are conducted by or originate from forces acting with hostile objectives.

This legal characterization allows for the timely recognition of misuse actions and their distinction from actions that do not constitute enemy activity through proper political and political-operative evaluation of the diverse activities in the church sector. It also forms the basis for targeted evidentiary measures to uncover, prevent, and combat church misuse. Misuse actions with high social danger, which are directed against the political, ideological, military, and economic foundations of the socialist state and legal order as a whole, are part of political underground activity. These actions are often characterized by a combination of conspiratorial means and methods with publicly effective and seemingly legal actions. Misuse actions that do not exhibit this high social danger but, as socially inappropriate, oppositional, or hostile-negative behaviors, have real connections to political underground activity in their practical-political consequences and development tendencies and can transform into it, are considered part of the prelude to → political underground activity.

Circumstantial Evidence

The process of proving the objective truth of insights about a politically-operative and, if necessary, legally significant matter to be clarified, exclusively based on indirect → evidence (→ indications) using a chain of circumstantial evidence; proving the truth in the process of → evidence presentation based on indirect evidence.

1. The result of the process of proving the objective truth based on indirect evidence in political-operative work and criminal proceedings; the proof of truth based on indirect evidence.

The circumstantial evidence is provided when, as a result of forming a chain of circumstantial evidence, the compelling conclusion is reached that the truth of an insight is established with objective certainty, i.e., when, due to the completeness and consistency of the chain of circumstantial evidence, it is impossible to reasonably doubt the truth of this insight, as every other plausible explanation can be ruled out with certainty.

Complex Assignment

An assignment to one or more unofficial collaborators (IM) aimed at realizing certain constant political-operative tasks and meeting a relatively constant complex informational need (e.g., exploring regime questions during border crossing into non-socialist foreign countries, monitoring the current whereabouts of members of Western military liaison missions, politically-operative securing of protocol routes for leading representatives and their guests, etc.). Each complex assignment must be checked for relevance in the event of significant changes in the political-operative situation and, if necessary, altered, improved, or withdrawn.

Compromising Material

Facts from a person's life that contradict societal (legal, moral) norms and views, and whose disclosure could lead to legal or disciplinary sanctions, loss of prestige, public exposure, risk to reputation within their social circle, and thus create or awaken the internal need in the person to avert the resulting negative consequences or rectify the damage caused. The effort to gain new unofficial collaborators (IM), to break individuals away from enemy groups, or to carry out → decomposition measures using compromising material, utilizes these existing or induced → need for security and reparation. Solving these tasks, especially with individuals with entrenched anti-socialist attitudes, may also require the creation of effective compromising material.

Compromising facts can include:

- Unaddressed legal violations,
- Breaches of duty, promotion of misconduct, and causing harm,
- Transgressions of moral and political-ideological norms,
- Concealment of incriminating personal connections, falsifications.

The motivating effect of compromising material is always tied to the individual. This effect is primarily dependent on:

- Ideological-moral attitudes, legal awareness, responsiveness, and character sensitivity,
- The person's social status and the associated public reputation,
- The professional position and behavioral norms applicable to the professional group the person belongs to,
- The norms of the group or circle to which the person feels they belong,
- The role of family relationships and the person's position regarding their relatives.

The use of compromising material must be differentiated depending on the person and its nature by:

- Compact application, e.g., to make individuals with hardened hostile attitudes aware of the seriousness of the situation,
- Selective, partial application, e.g., to give the person impulses for independent statements,
- Avoiding direct use, e.g., to develop positive attitudes towards the MfS in the person.

The effect of compromising material on the willingness to cooperate with the MfS is usually time-limited. Therefore, in working with IMs gained based on security and reparation needs, growing trust in the MfS and recognition of the necessity of unofficial work must gradually replace these motivations.

Conflict

The temporary sharp clash of opposing concerns, interests, or tendencies (conflict situation) or the concentrated, intensified form of resolving contradictions in political, ideological, economic, social, and psychological areas. Conflicts of these various kinds can express class struggle and forms of developmental contradictions that may also arise in shaping socialist society. They always indicate the particular severity of social and political confrontation and the risk of escalation and expansion and must, therefore, be carefully monitored and assessed in political-operative analysis of social processes. When incompatible, opposing motives, goals, or intentions converge in a person's life situation, it results in a psychological conflict experience, characterized by the person's temporary inability to decide between the available alternatives, leading to behavioral disruptions and psychological tensions and shocks. Conflicts must be expected and addressed within the MfS, especially with unofficial collaborators (IM) recruited based on security and reparation motives; with conspiratorially hostile individuals; and also among MfS members due to stark contradictions between performance prerequisites and requirements.

Confrontation

A method of investigative work to recognize and prove the objective truth. The confrontation aims to obtain evidence in the form of statements from the accused and witnesses.

Types:

1. Confrontation to verify statements and clarify contradictions in the statements of the accused and witnesses. For this purpose, two witnesses, two accused, or a witness and an accused can be confronted. This special form of interrogation must be well-prepared and conducted prudently by the investigators.

2. Confrontation for the purpose of identifying individuals. The sought person should be presented to the witnesses or the accused in a group (3-5 people) of outwardly similar individuals, with conditions similar to those under which the relevant acquaintance occurred (lighting and viewing conditions, clothing, carried items, movement of the person, etc.).

Contact Ability

An operationally significant personality trait for establishing and consolidating contact with operatively interesting persons. Contact ability is especially required in unofficial collaborators (IM) to overcome operatively interesting persons' deliberate restraint, possible insecurity, or enemy conspiracy measures. Contact ability can be developed in IMs through repeated, practice-based contact establishment. Contact ability is closely related to willingness to contact and → adaptability.

Control

A process in leading political-operative work to verify whether the requirements derived from the decisions and documents of the party and state leadership, official regulations and directives of the MfS, and the political-operative situation align with the course and results of political-operative work. Control contributes to creating a realistic picture of the quality and quantity of political-operative work and serves the leader's targeted influence on the realization of political-operative tasks by subordinate employees and the development of new, further political-operative goals and tasks. Control has the following main tasks:

- Monitoring the realization of political-operative tasks,
- Assessing and visualizing the work results of employees and the effectiveness of political-operative work,
- Creating well-founded bases for the leader's decisions, timely providing information for the leader's work and higher leadership

levels to generalize positive experiences and avoid errors and deficiencies in work,
- Constantly monitoring the observance of conspiracy, secrecy, and security,
- Constantly assessing cadres to timely initiate measures for their qualification and education.

Implementing these tasks according to the control's fundamental objective is only possible by ensuring the unity of guidance and control in leadership activity.

Corruption

A behavior foreign to socialism, contrary to its legal order, and harmful to society. Corruption involves both determining individuals to engage in harmful actions using their unilateral, individualistic personality traits directed towards satisfying excessive material needs or anti-socialist goals by offering, promising, or granting gifts or other advantages and the acceptance, promise, or demand for gifts or other advantages by individuals for realizing their harmful actions. Corruption-related favoritism and the associated pursuit of advantages usually involve breaches of duty. Imperialist intelligence services, other hostile entities, and forces use corruption to organize and conduct various forms of subversive activities against the socialist state and society. Imperialist intelligence services use corruption to recruit agents and establish strong ties with them. Representatives of capitalist enterprises commit corruption mainly to gain and expand personnel → bases in the DDR's economy to achieve state-hostile goals and obtain commercial and other economic advantages. Legal bases for combating corruption are §§ 247, 248 StGB, § 19 OWVO.

Counteraction

A specific form of operative play. Against recognized or suspected subversive activities of intelligence services or other hostile entities, complex operative measures are initiated to keep the subversive actions under control, document them, and offensively combat them.

The specificity of counteraction lies in reinforcing the enemy entities and individuals in their assumption that they have deceived the MfS, thus creating opportunities to learn about the plans and intentions pursued by them, as well as their means and methods, and to paralyze them.

Counterintelligence Work, Politically-Operative

The entirety of preventive, damage-preventing, offensive, focus-oriented, complex, and coordinated official and unofficial politically-operative activities of the operational lines and service units of the MfS to protect peace, secure and strengthen the DDR and its citizens from all enemy attacks inside and outside the DDR, and to ensure the socialist construction, especially the main task in its unity of economic and social policy, the consolidation of the socialist state community under the leadership of the USSR based on and in implementation of the decisions of the party and state leadership, the instructions and orders of the minister, in close cooperation with other protection and security organs, state organs, organizations, and institutions of the DDR, socialist and other states. It is an integrated part of the overall system of protection and security of the DDR and socialism.

The politically-operative counterintelligence work primarily serves

- the implementation of the security policy of the party, ensuring the state security of the DDR, protecting socialism, defending the power of the workers and peasants, and securing peace and associated security requirements,
- the timely and comprehensive detection and clarification as well as thwarting of plans, programs, intentions, machinations, measures, and activities directed against the DDR in the area of disruptive activities against the socialist economy, politically-ideological diversion, contact policy and contact activities,

organizing and inspiring political underground activities, creating a so-called internal opposition, organizing and inspiring citizens of the DDR to unlawfully leave the republic, state-hostile human trafficking, terrorist attacks and other state crimes, intelligence activities through espionage, especially military and economic espionage, as well as the creation of enemy bases and agencies including the misuse of citizens against the DDR,

- uncovering the causes and favorable conditions for state crimes and crimes of general criminality as well as other socially dangerous or socially adverse phenomena in the DDR and their overcoming, strengthening socialist legality, legal security and order, especially order, discipline and security in all social areas, maintaining secrecy and protecting secrets including raising the level of conspiracy and revolutionary vigilance,

- supporting the Marxist-Leninist party and its organs as well as the state organs, organizations and institutions in the DDR and their activities in further building the developed socialist society in the DDR through preventive and offensive combating of the enemy inside and outside the German Democratic Republic. Decisive prerequisites for effective counterintelligence work are

- the continuous qualification of scientific leadership and management activities to fulfill the security tasks arising from social development and class struggle as well as to develop the priorities of politically-operative counterintelligence work through qualified assessment of the operational situation conditions, the politically-operative situation, the main attack directions of the enemy, his activities including the effectiveness of enemy activities in all security areas,

- the trusting official and unofficial cooperation with the workers and their differentiated involvement in solving the tasks of counterintelligence work, especially increasing the effectiveness

and efficiency in working with the operational base and the targeted use of the IM to work against the enemy,
- the targeted and creative cooperation with other protection and security organs, state and economic leading organs, organizations and institutions in preventive and offensive counterintelligence work,
- the effective use and application of all politically-operative means and methods for successfully combating the enemy.

Counterrevolution

Class struggle by reactionary classes against the revolutionary struggle of progressive classes and layers. The goal of counterrevolution is to crush revolutionary movements, reverse the achievements of a revolution, and especially change the power question in favor of reactionary classes. Through counterrevolution, historically outdated classes try to forcibly halt the lawful societal development. Forms and methods of counterrevolution are highly diverse: reactionary uprisings, triggering civil wars, coups, revolts, conspiracies, individual terror, attempts at economic and political-ideological subversion (→ political-ideological subversion, economic → disruptive activities, political → underground activities), etc. To achieve their goals, internal and international reaction work closely together. In the era of transition from capitalism to socialism, revolution and counterrevolution clash with particular sharpness. Counterrevolution is the content and main goal of imperialism's strategy. In socialist countries, the socio-economic and class basis for counterrevolution has been eliminated. Socialism has achieved profound changes in the international balance of power in its favor. Acting from a deep defensive position, imperialism intensifies its subversive activities closely linked to its confrontation course and interference policy. The intelligence services and other organs and organizations of the imperialist power apparatus try to inspire and mobilize hostile-negative forces in socialist countries to political underground activities and numerous other hostile-negative actions and to organize and unite them into an ideological, personal, and organizational basis - a so-called "internal opposition" for the planned decomposition and destruction of socialism "from within." The fight against counterrevolution must be resolutely led by the Marxist-Leninist party at the head of all anti-imperialist forces, mainly through the socialist state. In doing so, socialist state security organs bear a very high and growing responsibility for timely uncovering and preventively, offensively crushing hostile plans.

Counter-Terrorism

A system of political and operational goals, tasks, and measures aimed at detecting, preventing, addressing, and combating terrorist and other operationally significant → acts of violence. Key components of MfS counter-terrorism include:

- Continuous assessment of terrorist and other operationally significant acts of violence as part of the operational situation assessment within the area of responsibility, to identify and determine the requirements for preventive counter-terrorism and the level of deployable operational forces, means, and methods.
- Developing and implementing tasks and measures to prepare and equip the operational forces for the successful detection, prevention, addressing, and combating of terrorist and other operationally significant acts of violence.
- Specifically directing operational processes, particularly immediate measures, the handling of operational cases, and the OPK towards detecting, preventing, addressing, and combating terrorist and other operationally significant acts of violence.
- Deploying operational forces to search for signs of emerging and developing terrorist and other operationally significant acts of violence and their precursor actions, incidents, and phenomena.

- Preventive security of persons and objects requiring special protection in the state's interest.
- Political and operational work within and after the operational area to timely detect plans, intentions, and measures directed against the DDR and other socialist countries by imperialist intelligence services and other hostile, particularly terrorist and other extremist centers, organizations, groups, and forces, as well as the means and methods used to carry out terrorist and other operationally significant acts of violence.
- Politically and operationally investigating incidents involving ongoing and completed terrorist and other operationally significant acts of violence.
- Deploying non-structural specifically trained or central structural forces to combat terrorist and other operationally significant violent offenders with military-operational means and methods on the orders of the responsible superior or the Comrade Minister.

Covert Apartment

An apartment (or room) provided to the MfS by an → unofficial collaborator (IM) to ensure conspiracy and communication (IMK/KM). Meetings are conducted in the covert apartment while ensuring the protection, conspiracy, and security of the IM. The established measures for disguising meetings in the covert apartment must be systematically and conscientiously enforced, involving its owner. Particularly through periodic checks of the owner and their family and the surroundings of the covert apartment, the conditions for its continued use are to be determined, and decisions about further use are made if there are indications of deconspiration or risks to the conspiracy. To ensure conspiracy, it is further necessary to ensure that only verified and reliable IMs meet in the covert apartment, appropriate to the objective conditions and acceptable numbers, with a specific documentation kept.

Crime

A general term for legal violations in the form of socially dangerous (→ social danger) and socially harmful (→ social harm) actions described as crimes in the Criminal Code and specific criminal laws. Crime is differentiated into three main groups according to its social nature, socio-economic causes, attack directions, and objectives:

- Crime endangering peace, directed against the sovereignty of the DDR, humanity, and human rights (cf. Chapter 1 - Special Part of the StGB),
- State-hostile crime (cf. Chapter 2 - Special Part of the StGB),
- General crime (cf. Chapters 3-9 - Special Part of the StGB and specific laws containing criminal provisions).

Crime; Relationship to Subversion

There are close relationships between → crime and the → subversion of the enemy, as → state crimes and politically-operative significant general crimes are inherent components of subversive enemy activities. Thus, the enemy increasingly aligns political-ideological subversion and enemy contact policy, essential parts of subversion, to create an ideological and personnel basis in the DDR, draw more individuals to hostile positions, and mobilize them for anti-socialist actions, including committing state crimes and politically-operative significant general crimes. The enemy uses state crimes, especially espionage, other treasonous crimes, state-hostile human trafficking, and politically-operative significant general crimes to accelerate subversive activities, undermine the trust between party and state leadership and the DDR population, influence DDR citizens in a hostile sense, and mobilize them for anti-socialist actions and discredit the international reputation of the DDR. The main group of crimes endangering peace, directed against the sovereignty of the DDR, humanity, and human rights, is part of the planning, preparation, and execution of aggression wars by imperialist forces against the DDR and other socialist community states.

Criminal Human Trafficking Group; Smuggling Methods

The covert methods practiced by human trafficking groups for the illegal transfer of people or goods out of the DDR's territory, violating legal provisions. The smuggling methods used by criminal human trafficking groups are highly diverse and continuously modified.

The most significant methods include:

The criminal and sometimes life-threatening smuggling of people in cars, trucks, and other cross-border transport vehicles, such as through the abuse of → transit traffic between the BRD and West Berlin, control-free traffic, and TIR agreements.

1. The misuse of identity documents from the BRD, other non-socialist countries, and West Berlin, including diplomatic passports, as well as the use of altered, forged, fake, or illegally issued documents, often in violation of international principles and norms and the sovereignty of numerous European countries.
2. The smuggling of people combined with acts of violence against the DDR's state border and those of other socialist countries, as well as terrorist attacks on border crossing points.
3. The search for and exploitation of gaps in the border security system, particularly in socialist countries, for the smuggling of DDR citizens.

Criminal Procedural Coercive Measure

An indispensable security measure or investigative action in the criminal procedure, restricting citizens' personal rights to the legally permissible extent and in the prescribed manner. The most significant criminal procedural coercive measures provided in the StPO are:

- Pre-trial detention (§ 122 ff. StPO)
- Preliminary → arrest (§ 125 StPO)
- Special supervision by guardians (§ 135 StPO)
- Bail (§ 136 StPO)
- Summoning of accused and defendants (§§ 48, 203, and 295 StPO)
- Bringing in suspects (§ 95 Abs. 2 StPO)
- Arrest during investigative actions (§ 107 StPO)
- Summoning of witnesses (§ 31 StPO)
- Search, account inspection, and seizure (§§ 108 ff. StPO)
- Monitoring and recording of telecommunications (§ 115 StPO)

The StPO specifies in detail the prerequisites for applying criminal procedural coercive measures, which criminal prosecution organ is responsible for applying them, and the formal requirements to be observed in their implementation.

Criminal procedural coercive measures individually aim to:

- Prevent the suspect, accused, or defendant from evading the procedure or the subsequent execution of the penalty, warning participants, or helping them escape, committing further offenses;

Ensure that existing and necessary evidence for → proof is identified and secured so that neither the owner nor the previous holder or other persons can legally dispose of it;

- Ensure that investigative actions are not disturbed, and orders of the criminal prosecution organ are followed.

In the → investigative work of the MfS, criminal procedural coercive measures are also used to:

- Identify all politically operative relevant contexts and processes in connection with the clarification of a crime or develop relevant clues;

- Support the proof process in the development and processing of operational personal controls and operational cases through the identification and securing of official evidence.

Criminalistic Traces

Material manifestations or materially fixed changes that are caused or left during the preparation, execution, or concealment of a crime or in connection with → political-operative incident and contain information about the crime or action. The inevitability of trace formation is based on scientific knowledge. They appear in various forms and are classified into the following categories according to their formation mechanism:

- Reproductive image traces,
- Original form traces,
- Substance and material traces,
- Situation traces (condition traces).

A specific area of traces defined by their size are → microtraces.

Traces are particularly important for operative work as carriers of operatively significant information and as evidence. The extraction of information from traces through operative trace evaluation and their analytical comparative examination by experts, as well as the means and methods of searching and securing traces, are subjects of criminalistic → traceology.

Cross-Border Traffic; Exit Ban

Type of → Travel Ban; state decision applied to citizens of the DDR or foreigners with permanent or long-term residence in the DDR, for whom reasons exist that would lead to serious damage to the reputation and interests of the DDR if they stayed abroad.

Exit bans are based on the Passport Law, Passport and Visa Regulations, and internal service regulations of the MdI and the MfS, are in accordance with international law, are international practice, and serve to enforce and implement the legal order of the DDR on its sovereign territory. They are an effective instrument of political-operational work to prevent subversive misuse of citizens of the DDR by the enemy and to ensure their protection and safety.

Requests for initiating exit bans must be submitted to the decision-making leaders with the necessary personal details and concrete justification of the evidence situation in accordance with the principles of travel bans.

Reasons for exit bans may exist for persons:

- Against whom an investigation procedure for committing a crime or a particularly serious offense has been initiated,
- Who still have to serve or compensate a legally binding sentence, provided that its execution does not take place in the home state, whose citizens they are,
- Who are previously convicted for another crime against the state order or another serious crime or have repeatedly committed offenses or whose probation period (this does not apply to foreigners) has not yet expired,
- About whom facts are known that suggest they would not represent the DDR in a worthy manner in other states, or there is a suspicion that the trip is intended to be used for illegal departure from the DDR,
- Where there is another threat to the interests of the DDR, especially the security interests of the DDR.

The implementation of exit bans is carried out by rejecting the application for exit in the → application, review, and decision procedure and through political-operational search measures. The duration of exit bans is to be determined depending on the reasons for initiation. In the absence of reasons, the immediate deletion of exit bans is to be carried out.

Cross-Border Traffic; Misuse Actions in Entry and Transit Traffic

Illegal activities committed by authorized participants in entry and transit traffic by exploiting the legitimate opportunities provided by the issuance of the permit to participate in entry and transit traffic.

For transit traffic between the BRD and West Berlin through the territory of the DDR, Article 16 of the Transit Agreement between the DDR and the BRD of December 17, 1971, contains a legal definition of misuse actions. They are aimed at realizing subversive and other plans, intentions, and measures that harm or endanger the interests of the DDR and its citizens.

The enemy attempts to exploit the opportunities created by international law regulations on entry and transit traffic, in violation of international law and the domestic law of the DDR, for organizing its subversive activities against the DDR and other socialist states, especially to intensify anti-state human trafficking and illegal border crossing, political-ideological diversion, contact policy and activities, intelligence activities, and other hostile activities, as well as to activate hostile forces in the DDR.

The tasks arising for the MfS to politically-operative secure entry and transit traffic place high demands on all operational service units and their coordinated cooperation and political-operative cooperation with other protection and security organs, other state organs, and social forces.

The focus of the political-operative security of entry and transit traffic is on preventing, uncovering, and combating hostile plans, intentions, and measures, ensuring safety and order on the territory of the DDR, and the contribution of the MfS to the safe and contract-compliant processing of entry and transit traffic.

Through the political-operative work of the MfS, among other things through the development of probative information/documentation on misuse actions in entry and transit traffic, a contribution is to be made for the purpose of preparing and supporting the implementation of propaganda, diplomatic, and other offensive political and international law-based measures (e.g., within the framework of the transit or traffic commission), the fundamental objective of which is to compel the government of the BRD or the Senate of West Berlin to consistently adhere to relevant international agreements and to take concrete measures against misuse actions and their inspirators and organizers.

The most important legal regulations and internal service regulations are:

- Treaty between the DDR and the BRD on Traffic Issues of May 26, 1972,
- Transit Agreement between the DDR and the BRD of December 17, 1971,
- Travel and Visitor Agreement between the Government of the DDR and the Senate of West Berlin of December 20, 1971,
- Order on the Entry of Citizens of the BRD into the DDR of October 17, 1972, and Order No. 2 of June 14, 1973, in the version of Order No. 3 of December 3, 1979,
- DA 3/75, 5/75, and 6/75 of the Minister for State Security,
- Service Regulation 40/74 of the Minister of the Interior and Chief of the DVP on Cross-Border Passenger Traffic of November 30, 1974.

Data Protection

The reliable protection of information stored on a physical data carrier, ensured by a system of coordinated legal, organizational, personnel, technical, and politically-operational measures, to keep it confidential in the interest of state and societal order. The goal of data protection is to secure the information comprehensively and uniformly and to create the necessary conditions for this. A particular focus for data protection is on operational and state bodies or persons who have access to such information. Data protection is closely related to confidentiality protection.

Deconspiracy

The revelation or uncovering of politically-operational working principles, goals and intentions, measures, forces, means, and facilities, which generally leads to significant endangerment of operational task realization, increasing political damage, loss of operational potential, or a substantial reduction in their effectiveness. The causes of deconspiracy are diverse, ranging from errors in operational actions to the effects of enemy activities to the influence of chance. Preventing deconspiracy requires particular attention to:

- Careless, schematic, routine-prepared and executed operational actions, especially violations of confidentiality and vigilance and source protection.
- Underestimating the danger, cunning, and efficiency of enemy activities and their counterintelligence agencies; failure to recognize targeted enemy provocations.
- Ideological misalignment, insufficient commitment to the MfS, inability to withstand enemy ideological pressure, resulting in attempts to avoid conspiratorial work.
- Insufficient politically-operational action preparation and unsuitability for certain work directions.

Demonstrative Offenders

Persons or groups who, out of various attitudes, goals, and motivations, intend to achieve high public visibility through their demonstrative-provocative behavior and thereby exert coercive pressure on the party and state leadership, state organs, social institutions, and their employees to enforce anti-socialist, illegal demands. Demonstrative offenders can be:

1. Hostile forces with entrenched anti-state attitudes, sometimes openly expressed. Anti-state motives and goals are the main elements in the conscious decision to act. They often operate under direct guidance from the opponent.
2. Other persons who, under the influence of political-ideological diversion, objectively align themselves with enemy efforts through their demonstrative-provocative behavior, without necessarily being fully aware of this connection. For these demonstrative offenders, the main motives and goals are primarily to enforce unjustified personal interests or demands.

Demonstrative-Provocative Behavior

Activities carried out by hostile forces or others acting under the influence or in the interest of the enemy, aimed at drawing public attention, demonstrating the opposition stance of these forces, or exerting blackmail pressure against the DDR (party and state leadership, central and local state organs, social institutions, and their employees) by mobilizing the broadest possible public to either force a decision in their favor or provoke reactions that burden the socialist state and social order in the class struggle and can be used by the enemy in further targeted hostile attacks, particularly in the context of politically-ideological diversion. Demonstrative-provocative behavior is part of the system of hostile activities, especially for organizing or inspiring → political underground activities in the DDR. In most cases, demonstrative-provocative behavior constitutes differentiated legal violations, ranging from state crimes, general criminal offenses to other types of legal violations, such as misconduct or administrative offenses, and endangers or impairs state or public order and security. It is often associated with

- attacks on political activities and decisions of the party in the class struggle with imperialism,
- attacks on measures and decisions of state organs,

- illegal attempts by DDR citizens to relocate to non-socialist states or West Berlin, etc., often preceded by massive, usually persistent demands, a threat of demonstrative-provocative behavior, or conspiratorial, long-term preparation.

The → demonstrators can act in direct cooperation with hostile forces. They choose methods, locations, and timing that they expect to have high mass impact, such as

- special class struggle situations or social events,
- the presence of representatives of Western mass media,
- appearing on central streets and squares, in front of buildings of the party and state leadership or local state organs, in front of diplomatic representations of capitalist states,
- displaying posters, writings, or symbols with openly inflammatory or covertly demagogic content,
- resistance actions against state measures related to preventing the behavior, etc.

Depth Security

The organization and implementation of continuous or temporary political-operational and military-tactical measures for the preventive security of spatially limited territories, areas, and sectors located in the immediate vicinity of security zones and restricted areas. Depth security aims to timely and preventively prevent the penetration of hostile and negative forces into the security zones and restricted areas, clarify the means and methods of the opponent, and recognize, eliminate, or limit crime-favorable conditions.

Depth security primarily also serves to recognize situational changes or situations that may pose a threat to security in the security zones and restricted areas. Depth security is carried out in close operational cooperation with other protection and security agencies based on concrete security concepts or coordination agreements.

Depth security is carried out along and within the depths of the restricted or border zones at the DDR's state borders, on transit routes, around important state, military, and economic objects, at central objects of party and state leadership, and at residential and recreational objects of leading representatives.

Depth security is implemented during concentrated military transports, movements of leading representatives of the DDR and their foreign guests by car, train, or ship, large events, and social highlights, especially when leading representatives participate and according to special instructions. In the context of depth security, official and unofficial forces, means, and methods, as well as operational security and surveillance technology, are deployed. The duration, territorial boundaries, and necessary force and means deployment are defined in confirmed agreements, action plans, or decisions.

Diplomatic Representations and Privileged Persons; Protection

An objective requirement of socialist foreign and security policy, a national task, and an expression of the DDR's and other states' international rights and obligations. The MfS's contribution, according to its responsibility and specific means and possibilities, is aimed at effectively supporting the offensive, coordinated foreign policy strategy and tactics of the socialist community of states and ensuring the DDR's interstate relations against disruptions and strains, considering the international trend of increasing terrorist and other attacks against diplomatic representations and privileged persons. This includes particularly increasing the MfS's effectiveness in the following main directions:

- Comprehensive uncovering of the plans, intentions, and measures of imperialist intelligence services, right- and left-wing extremist, and other hostile-negative forces to carry out terrorist, subversive, and other illegal attacks against diplomatic representations and privileged persons of the DDR or in the DDR.

- Ensuring high security, order, and discipline in the DDR's diplomatic foreign representations, including being well-prepared for terrorist, subversive, and other attacks against the DDR's foreign representations or their employees.
- Comprehensive and focused, i.e., corresponding to the differentiated foreign and security policy protection requirements, external security of representations, residences, and homes of privileged persons of the USSR, other socialist states, and other states in the DDR, and securing diplomatic events (protocol events).
- Processing specific protection requests directed to the DDR's organs by foreign representations and privileged persons, as well as other initial indications of possible, intended, or prepared terrorist and other attacks against representations and privileged persons and initiating immediate measures.

Particularly notable forms of terrorist and other attacks against representations and privileged persons are bomb attacks, embassy occupations, kidnappings, and hostage-takings. For preventive effectiveness, it is particularly important to ensure a constant, qualified political-operational situation assessment concerning increased protection requirements. This primarily involves considering the differentiated political importance of the respective interstate relations of the DDR, political highlights, tension situations, conflicts, and other conditions in the international arena, as well as within the various receiving or sending states, and the specific situation in the representations. International law obliges the DDR, among other receiving states, to prevent, uncover, and combat violent and other illegal attacks against the integrity or activities of diplomatic representations and privileged persons of other states under all conditions through appropriate measures and to cooperate in preventing and prosecuting corresponding crimes (see, among others, Art. 22, 29 of the Vienna Diplomatic Convention of 18 April 1961 and the Diplomatic Protection Convention of 14 December 1973).

These protection requirements extend to all representations and privileged persons granted diplomatic immunities and privileges under international law and the principle of reciprocity. These include primarily embassies, legations, consulates, official delegations, and other missions, as well as their heads, diplomatic staff, service staff, family members, and United Nations officials, their specialized organizations, and staff of the Warsaw Pact United Armed Forces.

Disinformation

Deliberate dissemination of information that fundamentally or partially contradicts the facts through word, writing, image, or actions. The MfS uses disinformation with the goal of:

- Deceiving hostile forces about its own plans, intentions, and measures, and concealing its own forces, means, and methods.
- Steering enemy activities and forces in directions favorable to the MfS or unsettling these forces to create conditions for carrying out its own measures, as well as identifying and paralyzing enemy forces, means, methods, attack directions, target objects, target groups, and target persons.

Disinformation must be effective and withstand scrutiny for as long as necessary to accomplish the specific task. Therefore, the informational content of disinformation must seemingly logically derive from objective conditions or facts.

Launching disinformation requires carefully coordinated, interdependent, and complementary measures and is usually part of → operational games. All operational forces, means, and methods of the MfS, potentials of other state organs and institutions, and social organizations can be utilized for this purpose. Politically-operational measures aimed at disinforming intelligence services, enemy leadership centers, committees, organizations, and institutions require the approval of the responsible main department. The enemy's intelligence services and other centers of subversive activity use disinformation to:

- Deceive the security and intelligence agencies of the DDR and other socialist states about their own plans and intentions.
- Provoke desired activities to their own advantage.
- Manipulate the consciousness of their own country's population using all mass media and act subversively against socialist scouts.
- Influence the leadership centers of other, non-socialist states in their favor.

Dissident

Latin for "someone who thinks differently," "someone who believes differently." A term deliberately chosen by the opponent for persons in socialist states who fundamentally oppose the worldview of the working class and the social practice in socialist countries and publicly act with corresponding intentions and actions, partly by consciously circumventing or abusing the possibilities of socialist democracy.

The use of this term aims to suggest a "broad internal opposition" and "underground movement" in socialist countries. According to this objective, the opponent labels both state criminals and criminal, decadent, asocial, religiously bound, and other persons who do not agree with the worldview of the working class and the social practice in socialist countries as dissidents, to declare them "political opponents" of socialism and assign them to a "broad internal opposition."

Document Examination

A criminalistic method involving visual-optical, metrological, physical-chemical, and other examinations of documents. The subject of document examination is records (documents) created in the exercise of state and social functions, in the exercise of official or other professional powers, in the exercise of personal rights and obligations, or otherwise, and can testify to operationally significant or criminally relevant circumstances.

Documents include passports, IDs, certificates, letters, but also anonymous and pseudonymous hate and threat writings, hostile-negative concepts, and examples of so-called "underground literature." Documents are created by hand or machine writing, printing, or other methods mainly involving the application of colored substances. Their carrier material is usually paper. To organize the variety of documents encountered in politically-operational practice, in addition to genuine documents whose comprehensive operational evaluation is paramount and which are also used as comparison materials, the following categories of operationally significant documents can be summarized:

- Altered documents: created from mostly genuine documents through erasures, additions, cover-ups, or other deliberate manipulations.
- Imitated documents: entirely new creations based on genuine documents, striving for maximum similarity to the original.
- Fictitious documents: often resembling commonly used genuine documents and appearing realistic but invented in design, execution, etc.
- Unlawfully issued documents: so-called blank documents from original print runs with unauthorized entries, imprints of imitated seals and stamps, etc.
- Documents of unknown origin and manufacturing method: mainly grouped under the aspect of searching for the author or manufacturer.

The goal of document examination is to obtain conclusive information about the presence of altered, imitated, fictitious, or unlawfully issued documents and the materials, tools, and other aids used to create or forge them, as well as information about hostile-negative individuals who may have appeared as authors, manufacturers, or users of the operationally relevant documents. Document examination includes the operational assessment and evaluation of documents, which can be carried out using simple technical aids, such as magnifying glasses, UV lamps, templates, by appropriately trained operational employees, and the → expertise conducted by experts and specialists using special techniques and procedures. The following examinations are primarily conducted:

- Determining alterations made, such as photo substitutions, erasures, additions, etc.
- System determination and identification of typewriters based on existing writing performances.

→ Identification of stamps, stamp types, and seals based on their imprints.

- Determining the manufacturing method of printing and duplication products.
- Authenticity examination of polygraphic products.
- Determining and comparing writing substances (inks, ballpoint pen pastes) and writing tools.
- Examination of adhesives and glues on documents.
- Deciphering or restoring smudged, erased, or faded records, deciphering blind impressions.
- Restoring records on burnt paper.
- Determining the type of paper.
- Identifying a previously connected document from its parts.
- Dating documents or individual elements thereof.

Double Agent

A spy for one intelligence service who, under the cover of apparent unofficial cooperation with the MfS, carries out subversive tasks assigned by their employer against the MfS. The hostile activities of double agents are directly aimed at the politically-operational capability, combat effectiveness, and reliability of the MfS. Fundamental goals and attack directions of double agents include:

- Systematically exploring the plans, intentions, and measures of the MfS.
- Detecting and exposing scouts in the operational area and unofficial forces, means, and methods to gain starting points for targeted subversive attacks against the MfS.
- Investigating and processing MfS members and their families and acquaintances with the intention of conducting recruitments for direct penetration into the MfS through compromise and subversion or gathering and using compromising material to obtain classified information about the security organs and other societal areas, as well as about the party and state leadership's strategy and tactics through intelligence gathering or preparing targeted acts of treason.
- Identifying official and covert MfS objects to identify MfS members or IM and create starting points for further processing.
- Disorienting the work of the security organs to paralyze combat effectiveness, especially in conflict situations, or to thwart the MfS's intentions and measures by diverting from the realization of main tasks.

The main methods of creating double agents include:

- Infiltrating spies into MfS offices, institutions, and facilities with which the MfS maintains official contacts, and into MfS members, their relatives and acquaintances, and unofficial forces.
- Recruiting IM operating in the operational area.

Eastern Research

A means of the aggressive, counterrevolutionary policy of imperialism directed against the socialist community of states and the growing influence of real socialism on the population of imperialist states to analyze developments taking place in real socialism, develop counterrevolutionary concepts directed against the socialist states, and anti-communist role models to manipulate the population of imperialist states. As a significant concept-forming and ideology-producing area of the imperialist ruling system, Eastern research occupies an important place in the extensive system of subversive activities of imperialism against the socialist states, closely linked with the espionage activities of imperialist intelligence services and numerous other hostile organizations.

In connection with the growing compulsion of imperialism to adapt to its changed conditions of existence and the resulting modifications of its counterrevolutionary strategy and tactics, Eastern research is also subject to changes in its functions and tasks, organization, and the means and methods it uses.

Originally focused only on the study of Eastern European countries, imperialist Eastern research particularly changed and expanded in connection with the re-profiling of psychological warfare and the formation of the system of → political-ideological diversion in the 1950s within the framework of Cold War policy.

From the mid-1950s to the early 1960s, "Sovietology" emerged as a new "scientific discipline" within Eastern research, whose research subject was Marxism-Leninism and the communist world movement on a global scale.

In the wake of the defeat of the aggressive and counterrevolutionary post-war policy directed at incorporating the DDR into the sphere of control of BRD imperialism and the beginning shift to a long-term, gradual "softening" and "undermining" of the foundations of the socialist social order and the counterrevolutionary undermining of political power relations in the DDR, "DDR research" was developed as a relatively independent branch of BRD imperialism's Eastern research in the second half of the 1960s.

In the conception and implementation of the BRD imperialism's policy towards the DDR under the neo-revanchist doctrine of "keeping the German question open," "DDR research," in close connection with intelligence services and other institutions of the imperialist ruling system, has important tasks to fulfill. The "Eastern and DDR research" of the BRD is firmly integrated into the system of hostile activities and creates essential prerequisites for organizing and carrying out the subversive activities of the enemy against the socialist countries.

Functions of Eastern research are:

- Analyzing and evaluating developments taking place in the socialist community of states in political, economic, military, and cultural areas to derive targeted measures for organizing and carrying out subversive attacks against the socialist states to realize the counterrevolutionary concept of long-term softening, undermining, and elimination of socialism,
- Developing anti-communist role models used to manipulate the population of their own country or for psychological warfare and political-ideological diversion against the socialist states,
- Actively assisting in implementing Eastern policy by participating in the planning staffs of the state-monopolistic ruling system, participating in the political-ideological field, and cooperating with imperialist intelligence services.

The increased significance of Eastern research in the anti-communist concept of imperialism is expressed in the creation of state leadership bodies and institutions for the staff leadership of Eastern research and its effectiveness. The main imperialist powers strive at the state level for coordination of their Eastern research and the exchange of "research results."

Economic Disruption Activities

A part of the subversive activities of imperialism within the system confrontation against socialism to implement the imperialist strategy of changing internal power relations in socialist countries. It is inspired and organized by imperialist intelligence services, other entities and forces outside the DDR, hostile personal bases in capitalist corporations, banks, and enterprises to undermine or re-profile the DDR's economy so that it fits into the imperialist economic framework, ultimately achieving the gradual restoration of capitalist production relations. It is carried out by hostile personal bases or other hostile forces in the form of a complex of activities involving economic damage and disruptions, material and personnel infiltration, particularly in growth-determining areas, projects, and processes of the DDR's economy and socialist economic integration. The imperialist centers and forces aim to achieve the following subversive goals through economic disruption activities:

- Material and personnel penetration into development-determining areas, projects, and processes of the DDR's economy and socialist economic integration to disrupt, hinder, or completely undermine them in the long term,
- Through hostile personal bases or other hostile forces, loosening the DDR's relations with the USSR and other countries of the socialist community as a key prerequisite for politically and economically undermining the DDR,
- Creating hostile-negative ideological positions to effectively work against the leading role of the party, the unity of the socialist community of states, and achieve a relaxation of the political situation and transformation of the socialist social system towards rapprochement with imperialist states,

- Developing, producing, and maintaining extensive dependencies of individual socialist countries on imperialist states to create a re-profiling of the socialist economic structure that aligns with the production profile of multinational corporations,
- Enlightening and penetrating the economic and scientific-technical cooperation of socialist countries with anti-imperialist countries to disrupt, discriminate against, and ultimately convert them to imperialist interests.

The externally initiated and organized activities of economic disruption appear in various forms: direct interference and political blackmail of socialist countries by misusing existing economic and scientific-technical relations, open breaches of contracts and agreements, non-recognition of international practices and trade customs, especially the principle of most-favored-nation status and mutual benefit by imperialist government circles.

Developing hostile-negative ideological positions and creating an internal opposition, particularly in people's enterprises and economic leading organs of the DDR, to instigate actions undermining, falsifying, or failing to implement the resolutions of the party and state leadership of the DDR. The expanding efforts to obtain comprehensive information through harvesting, espionage, and unauthorized disclosure from the DDR's economy and socialist economic integration through the increased use of imperialist intelligence services, corporate intelligence services, foreign correspondents, and Eastern research institutions as a fundamental prerequisite for initiating targeted restrictions and embargo measures and organizing direct disruption and economic undermining measures against the DDR's economy. Organizing direct disruptions in the reproduction process through immediate, damage-causing actions and targeted poaching of skilled workers to create difficulties and obstacles in the DDR's economic development. Infiltrating areas and processes of the economy to exploit the DDR's economic and scientific-technical potential for imperialist purposes and re-profiling important branches of the economy so that it is possible to align and eventually integrate them into the economic structure of capitalist industrial countries.

Electronic Warfare

English: Electronic warfare - commonly known: ELOKA. A term coined by Western military forces for an allegedly legitimate form of modern military combat by NATO powers in times of peace and war, particularly against socialist states, through the use of an extensive system of electronic devices. In essence, however, it is a complex system of electronic espionage. Electronic warfare aims to obtain information from all societal areas, strategically and tactically reconnoitre and disrupt communication systems in target countries, and implement own protective measures. The central planning, preparation, organization, and evaluation of the results of electronic warfare is conducted by imperialist intelligence services.

Encryption

The alteration of the form of a message for the purpose of confidentiality by transforming the commonly used representation into another form. The type and extent of the alteration of a message are based on an agreement between the sender and receiver through different assignments of the letters of the alphabet, by converting letters and words into numbers or groups of numbers or vice versa, as well as in other forms. The assignment in one direction is called encryption, the reverse is decryption. A message transmitted in the commonly used representation without encryption is referred to in intelligence parlance as a message sent in clear text.

Enemy

Individuals who, in groups or individually, deliberately develop political-ideological attitudes and views alien to socialism and seek to realize these attitudes and views through their practical behavior by intentionally causing events or conditions that endanger or damage the socialist state and social order generally or in specific aspects.

Enemy Band

A group of hostile-negative persons inspired or organized by the opponent, especially by imperialist intelligence services, relatively stable and existing over a longer period of time. Enemy bands are characterized mainly by the division of labor, coordinated, and mutually dependent actions of several individuals based on a unified criminal overall plan for the continuous commission of hostile actions. The particular danger of enemy bands lies, among other things, in the frequent use of dangerous and brutal means and methods in the implementation of their subversive activities. The inspiration, formation, and organization of armed enemy bands have always been part of the imperialist arsenal to achieve counter-revolutionary goals in socialist states or young national states. Enemy bands are mainly used by the opponent in crisis situations to commit acts of aggression, terrorist attacks against progressive persons or property, and other hostile actions. The organization or promotion of enemy bands to commit acts of aggression against the territorial integrity or political independence of the DDR or another state constitutes the offense of preparing and conducting acts of aggression according to § 86 StGB. Enemy bands also include → criminal human trafficking bands as inspirers and organizers of anti-state human trafficking according to § 105 StGB.

Enemy Manipulation

A specific method of ideological influence on the masses, aimed at eliminating or channeling their active, independent-creative activity into system-compliant paths through mental disintegration, deformation, and uniformity of thinking. It is one of the methods for maintaining state-monopolistic class rule and is directed against all revolutionary main forces of the present. Domestically, it aims to integrate the working class and all other working classes and strata into the state-monopolistic rule system. Its goal is to degrade citizens to externally controlled objects, educate them into anti-communists and compliant subjects who support the maintenance of the ruling system, endure economic exploitation and political oppression patiently, and view the pseudo-ideals of this system as their own.

Contrary to their objective class interests, people are to be aligned with the ideology of the ruling monopoly bourgeoisie in their worldview, thinking habits, feelings, aesthetic judgments, and entire way of life without being aware of it. The method of manipulation builds on a specific basic pattern of already internalized bourgeois role models, moral norms, thought schemes, and habits of bourgeois lifestyle. It abuses certain regularities of the human cognitive process and other scientific results from sociological, psychological, and psychiatric research. Manipulation particularly prefers influencing the emotional area or the subconscious and usually occurs in such a way that the resulting behavior appears as the "freely" chosen decision of the affected persons. Its main method lies in operating with half-truths, attaching to insignificant, incidental phenomena, and constantly repeating unproven assertions, lies, and slanders.

As an instrument of imperialist foreign policy, manipulation mainly attempts to influence citizens of other states of the imperialist world system, the national liberation movement, and especially the socialist community in a differentiated and targeted manner through mass media. The direct or indirect influence on the consciousness content of citizens of socialist countries aims to bring them into conflict with the socialist state and social order and, based on this, to misuse them for enemy activities (→ political-ideological diversion).

A specific target of enemy manipulation is to undermine the ideological and political basis of any cooperation with socialist security organs and to recruit people for active enemy activities of imperialist intelligence services. For this purpose, a distorted, false image of socialist reconnaissance activity is drawn, agent psychosis and espionage hysteria are stirred up. This creates reservations, insecurity, etc., which must be considered in political-operational work.

The impact of enemy manipulation should neither be underestimated nor overestimated. The growing appeal of real socialism, the victorious advance of the scientific worldview of Marxism-Leninism, the progress of all anti-imperialist forces, and the deepening and intensification of inner-imperialist contradictions set limits to it.

Enemy object

An enemy object is a state, social, or private institution or establishment in the operational area that is constantly or temporarily engaged in subversive activities within the system of hostile activities. The main task of political-operative work in and after the operational area is to investigate and handle such enemy objects. These objects are of particular interest because they concentrate secret information about the plans and intentions, means, and methods of the enemy against socialism and its allies.

Combating these enemy objects can deliver significant blows to the enemy. Handling them can create starting positions for penetrating further, particularly protected enemy objects. Additionally, their handling is crucial for ensuring the security of operative work. Therefore, handling enemy objects must create the conditions for conducting far-reaching offensive or political-operative measures against the enemy.

Enforcement of State Authority

Measures to ensure and guarantee the respect and recognition of state organs and their political, economic, military, social, legal, cultural, and other actions and determinations. The enforcement of state authority includes the consistent implementation of state decisions and the use of state-legal means, including actions against violators. It is realized through the executive and administrative activities of state organs in political, economic, military, social, legal, cultural, and other areas. The enforcement of state authority aims to further solidify social relations between the power organs of the socialist state and the working people, thereby increasing state authority. The enforcement of state authority relies on decisive objective factors such as:

- The secured political power of the working class,
- The leadership of state organs by the Marxist-Leninist party,
- The objective alignment of societal and individual interests.

And subjective factors such as:

- The scientifically qualified work of state organs,
- The party-like, class-conscious appearance of their employees,
- The closest connection to the working people,
- The knowledge and joint solution of all state and social problems and the personal matters of the working people.

Their further development, formation, and solidification are decisive foundations for the enforcement of state authority. The continuous enforcement of state authority is an essential requirement and a crucial prerequisite for solving state tasks in all social areas, carried out by state organs in realization of party resolutions and resulting and underlying laws, regulations, and other legal provisions.

The main method of enforcing state authority is the political-ideological influence on the working people based on Marxism-Leninism. This aims to educate citizens to consciously and voluntarily recognize state authority and enable them to actively support its enforcement. The enforcement of state authority demands the active participation of citizens in shaping state and social life. All state organs are responsible for enforcing state authority. The actions of all state organs collectively ensure the enforcement of state authority internally and externally. The work of the MfS is an essential part of ensuring the enforcement of state authority and contributes significantly to its enforcement through effective politically-operative work and targeted public relations.

Espionage

A state crime according to §§ 97 and 98 of the StGB (Criminal Code). It is part of the system of hostile activities against the DDR and other socialist states. Espionage is committed to the detriment of the interests of the DDR for a foreign power, their institutions or representatives, an intelligence service, or foreign organizations and their helpers by collecting, betraying, delivering, or otherwise making confidential information or items accessible.

Espionage is primarily characterized by the following features:

- It is a crucial means of shaping and realizing the aggressive policies of imperialism and increasingly influences the decision-making of the governments of imperialist states, particularly through the manipulation of such decisions. The imperialist states thus exert a decisive, coordinating influence in organizing and directing espionage. The espionage activities of imperialist intelligence services are increasingly coordinated within NATO to enforce their aggressive strategy.
- It is primarily directed against the internal and external security of the DDR, against the socialist community of states, but also against national liberation movements and all progressive movements in capitalist countries.
- It serves the main imperialist powers to infiltrate, hinder, and disrupt societal development in socialist countries and to divide the unity and cohesion of the socialist community of states, thereby creating conditions to enforce tactical variants of their struggle against the DDR and other countries of the socialist community and to achieve their illusory strategic goal of eliminating real socialism altogether.

It is an essential component of subversive activities and simultaneously a prerequisite and starting point for organizing, conducting, and escalating further subversive actions, particularly within the framework of externally inspired and organized political underground activities, including state crimes (→ political-ideological diversion, → contact policy/contact activities, economic → disruptive activities including sabotage, state-hostile human trafficking, and others).

- It is one of the most essential tasks of imperialist intelligence services, which infiltrate almost all aspects of societal life in capitalist countries and comprehensively exploit various state, social, and other organizations, institutions, and similar entities for espionage purposes.

It is aimed at obtaining → state and → official secrets. Particular importance is given to collecting information about the defense capabilities of the socialist community, their armed forces, new methods for protecting the population and troops from nuclear, biological, and chemical weapons, and priority nuclear strike targets in case of war. This is done in the interest of the most reactionary circles of the imperialist states united in NATO. They have not yet abandoned hope for achieving military superiority and attempt to spy on an opportune moment for armed conflict through espionage. Additionally, they are particularly interested in information from the economic sector, especially the defense industry, the basic and processing industries, existing, under construction, and planned industrial plants, resource extraction, the status and development prospects of the energy industry, transport, traffic, and communications, agriculture and food industry, trade, and the credit and finance sectors, as well as in the fields of science and technology.

- It is complexly directed against the political, economic, and military areas of the socialist social and state order and is committed, depending on the strategic and tactical plans and intentions of imperialism, primarily against selected focal points of these areas.

To realize the expanding objectives of espionage, a variety of sophisticated means and methods are applied, increasingly disguised, such as the use of recruited spies for self-exploration and → extraction of → secret holders and other individuals, subversive misuse of the status of diplomats and correspondents, organizing a comprehensive questioning system in non-socialist countries, evaluating official publications, using missiles, exploiting radio and electronic systems from one's own territory, and more.

Evidence Collection

Process of obtaining insights about a matter and proving their truth value (evidence).

In the politically-operational work of the MfS, evidence collection is the process led by orders, directives, and orientations of the Minister, generally oriented to legal regulations, for practical and theoretical activities to gain insights about politically-operationally significant incidents, matters, and persons, and proving their truth value. Insights and evidence must be documented objectively. Evidence collection in politically-operational work of the MfS is aimed at the credible determination of the objective truth of insights about the enemy, his plans and intentions, the means and methods he applies, any activities of hostile-negative persons and groups, as well as other politically-operationally significant matters and persons. It is a crucial basis for a realistic political-operational situation assessment, a key prerequisite for effective politically-operational measures to support the policy of the party and state leadership, and an important basis for scientifically grounded decision-making in the preventive prevention, detection, and combating of state crimes, politically-operationally significant crimes of general criminality, and other politically-operationally significant incidents, for the objective information of central and local party and state organs and for ensuring the constitutional rights of citizens.

Following the valid orders and directives in the MfS, evidence collection in politically-operational work is an essential part of checking initial clues, developing operational source materials, conducting operational personal controls when clarifying politically-operationally significant incidents, and processing operational cases and investigation cases. In consistent implementation and strict adherence to socialist legality, evidence collection in politically-operational work is primarily aimed at reliably clarifying politically-operationally and possibly legally relevant matters as well as politically-operationally interesting persons; this requires the use of all operational and criminalistic forces, means, and methods.

Evidence collection requires methodically correct procedures. The most important measures and thought operations of the evidence collection process are:

- Party-like and objective assessment of the political and politically-operational significance of the obtained evidence and information, evaluation of their possible legal relevance.
- Determining the subject of evidence collection, including its constant concretization and, if necessary, its redefinition.
- Purposeful search and professional securing of evidence as the objective basis of evidence collection.
- Objective evaluation of the information content of the evidence.
- Checking the truth value of the information obtained from the evidence needed for evidence collection.
- Assessment of the evidence and the entire evidence collection process concerning the subject of evidence collection.

In socialist criminal proceedings, evidence collection is regulated by detailed evidentiary provisions of criminal and criminal procedure law. These regulations, including the admissibility of evidence secured exclusively through criminal procedural means, must be observed already at the operational stage of evidence collection if a criminal proceeding or other official use of operationally achieved work results is intended.

Expert IM

→ Informal Collaborator for a Special Assignment (IME)

Expertise

Investigative and evaluative activity by experts and the resulting insights from this activity. In the political-operational work of the MfS, expertise is conducted whenever specific knowledge is required to clarify and investigate politically operationally significant occurrences or to clarify operationally relevant circumstances, and forensic and other scientific-technical facilities must be utilized.

Different types of expertise are distinguished, such as forensic, forensic medical, psychiatric, technical, agrotechnical, zootechnical, accounting, commodity, and other expertise. Objects of forensic expertise include primarily handwritten and typewritten documents, passports and other documents, weapons and ammunition, → suspicious explosive items, fingerprint traces, shoe, tire, and tool marks, parts of various objects, biological objects, substances, photographs, and more. One of the most important tasks of forensic expertise is establishing identity (→ person identification, → object identification).

The results of expertise are documented in written → expert reports, investigation or evaluation reports, and assessments, serving to support operational work. Expert reports can be used as evidence in criminal proceedings (§ 24 StPO). Due to their scientific content, they are often crucial information sources for reconstructing the crime and simultaneously providing grounds for proving the truth of these findings. Additionally, expert reports may include recommendations for preventing and avoiding legal violations (§ 38 StPO). The MfS's technical investigation unit is the primary facility for predominantly scientific-technical expertise. Outside the MfS, expertise can also be conducted under the protection of secrecy by the criminalistic institute (KI) of the Deutsche Volkspolizei or the criminal technology departments in the districts, the criminalistics section at Humboldt University, institutes and facilities at the universities of the DDR, and also other state institutions or reliable citizens with specialized knowledge due to extensive professional experience from all societal sectors (§ 29 StPO).

Fingerprinting

A method of criminal → personal identification based on the fact that the patterns of ridges on fingers/hands and the soles of feet are permanent and unique. In politically-operational work, the search, securing, and evaluation of fingerprint traces are to be carried out whenever persons have left traces during operationally significant actions or when it is likely that fingerprint traces are present at places/items to be investigated in the clarification of → politically-operational incidents. Comparison fingerprints required for comparative examination are usually obtained covertly by operational forces and measures.

The fingerprint traces secured in politically-operational work and the obtained comparison fingerprints are centrally recorded, classified, and stored. The fingerprint collection maintained by the MfS forms an important basis for recognizing and identifying hostile-negative forces and other operationally interesting persons.

An → expertise, resulting in the identification or exclusion of a person as the cause of fingerprint traces, makes a valuable contribution to increasing the quality of evidence collection.

Foreign flag

The core of a specific method of recruiting IM from the operational area. It is based on deceiving the recruitment candidate about the socialist relationship partner.

Its application allows the recruitment of candidates with consolidated anti-communist and reactionary attitudes and strong ties to their ruling system. The determination of the flag and the definition of its required scope and effort are determined by the operative possibilities and the personality of the recruitment candidate.

Full-time Security Officers

Officers on special duty of the MfS, deployed in significant areas of the national economy of the DDR to solve specific politically operative and economically important tasks, particularly to enforce order and security.

The activities of full-time security officers are aimed at contributing to the creative implementation and smooth fulfillment of the decisions of the party and state leadership in shaping the developed socialist society and ensuring that order and security are a firm part of leadership activities.

The tasks of security officers include:

- Preventing or uncovering and analyzing political and economic disruptive activities of enemy forces and causing the elimination of causes and favorable conditions,
- Contributing to the establishment and maintenance of order and security in the area of responsibility according to the legally regulated tasks and duties,
- Ensuring the preparation, implementation, and control of leader decisions in the field of order and security.

Security officers fulfill their tasks by:

- Supporting the leaders of state and economic organs in fulfilling their responsibility for ensuring order and security in the leadership areas of the national economy,
- Conducting inspection activities on behalf of the state leader in consultation with the MfS. Full-time security officers, as members of the respective enterprise or economic leading or state organ, are subject to the labor law regulations of the Labor Code and, as officers on special duty, to the military regulations of the MfS.

Security officers must continuously work on developing the skills and prerequisites required to fulfill their tasks. They must acquire comprehensive knowledge in Marxism-Leninism, socialist leadership science, scientific and technical and economic development in the area of responsibility, and socialist law and have politically operative basic training.

Grid

Term for an enemy instrument used to uncover socialist scouts, detect operative means and methods of socialist security agencies, and identify political opponents and individuals involved in general crime and terrorism. Grids are systems of characteristic features of defensive and security-relevant persons, items, objects, and situations in the form of fact sheets, card indexes, databases, etc., using the latest electronic data processing technology.

By systematically and purposefully analyzing matching features and providing corresponding tactical advice to executive bodies and segments of the population, grids become an essential tool for enemy control and counter-intelligence agencies in their search activities. For solving various counter-intelligence tasks to identify individuals, the enemy has developed different grids, such as:

- on intelligence means and methods,

- for recognizing suspicious behaviors, circumstances, and appearances,
- for monitoring cross-border traffic,
- for controlling vehicles,
- for securing specially protected objects.

Grids are continually updated and improved with new insights.

See also: Enemy Search System

Group Analysis, Operational

The process and result of the systematic and ongoing analysis of the character and nature of groups, which may be subject to operational work for various reasons.

Group analysis focuses on:

- The content of the group's common goals and tasks (including particularly: written programs and platforms in negative groups, but also, for example, state guidelines for positive groups, existing norms, values, and customs),
- The spatial and temporal conditions under which group life takes place (including particularly: the duration and frequency of meetings, the efforts made by individual members to participate in group meetings, the nature of the meeting place),
- The cooperation and communication among group members to achieve set goals (including particularly: factors that increase social danger in negative groups due to a division of labor or that enhance performance in positive groups, the establishment of stable conversational relationships (communication structure) between group members),
- The group structure, which is the expression of the diverse social relationships among group members and includes, for example: the functional structure derived directly from the specific task, naming individual functionaries (e.g., radio operators, drivers),

the rank structure, which reflects the typical contributions of group members to task fulfillment and characterizes leaders, active members, and followers, and the evaluation structure, which mirrors the emotional relationships among group members, such as sympathy and antipathy relationships, thus also expressing the overall group atmosphere.

These analytical aspects, which also describe a group as a specific form of a union of persons, allow for the assessment of operationally relevant situations such as the formation of groups, the current development status of groups, or the likely behavior of group members. This enables the derivation of measures for the targeted processing and securing of groups.

Habits

Personality traits for carrying out individual actions that occur frequently, resulting in automated, less conscious processes and including the need for their repeated execution. Elementary and complex habits occur regularly and consistently in all areas of life. Determining the habits of operatively interesting individuals allows relatively reliable conclusions about their individuality, → attitudes, and other characteristics.

The main significance lies in utilizing and developing favorable habits in IMs and social employees for political-operative work, such as securing meetings, regularly establishing contact from the IM to the employee, critically discussing every behavior line, fully mastering the rules for reporting, etc. The habituation process must be used as an operationally significant relief process that frees mental and volitional capacities for creatively solving political-operative tasks in operative and informal employees.

A prerequisite is to ensure that conscious, precise, and positively motivated learning of conspiracy rules is observed from the beginning in the formation of habits, which are solidified in later repetitions, exercises, behavior training, and practical use. The development of operationally useful habits must avoid the emergence of schematism and routine.

Hatred

Intense and deep feeling that can significantly influence people's actions. It always reflects opposing interpersonal relationships and is the emotional expression of irreconcilable class and interest contradictions between the working class and the bourgeoisie (class hatred) in social life. The moral content of hatred depends on the object it is directed at and can therefore be valuable and noble or petty and low.

Hatred always aims at active confrontation with the hated opponent, is not content with disgust and reporting, but is often associated with the desire to destroy or harm them. Hatred is a crucial component of Chekist feelings, one of the decisive foundations for the passionate and relentless fight against the enemy. Its strengthening and deepening in the practice of class struggle and a concrete and real → image of the enemy is the task and goal of class education. Hatred is also a lasting and powerful motive for action. It must therefore be consciously used and strengthened as a drive for difficult operative tasks in conspiratorial work.

Hostile activity; camouflage of

Hostile actions to carry out attacks against socialist society undetected by security organs and societal vigilance and avoiding confrontations with the norms of socialist law. Camouflage is thus a crucial element of the subversive nature of hostile activity.

Camouflage of hostile activity occurs:

- Through the use of intelligence means and methods to cover the actual nature and objectives of individuals, institutions, communication routes, and actions,

- Through legal positions and the misuse of state and societal institutions,
- Through actions outside or below criminal liability.

Revealing the camouflage serves to uncover hostile attacks and create identification features for the search for the enemy, politically exploit the misuse of state and interstate institutions and relationships, inspire societal vigilance, and orient towards current variants of hostile actions.

Hostile activity; combating of

Overall state-societal process aimed at ensuring → state security against the attacks carried out by the enemy on the constitutional foundations of the socialist state and social order.

Combating includes the entirety of the socialist state's and its organs' actions, social organizations, and forces, such as measures for prevention, uncovering, investigation, and prevention in their mutually conditioned unity against the enemy's attacks.

The predominantly conspiratorial approach of the enemy requires a special organ of the socialist state—the MfS—which, through targeted, concentrated, and priority-oriented political-operative work, fulfills specific tasks for the prevention, prevention, and uncovering of hostile activities based on the decisions of the party, the laws, and other legal provisions of the socialist state, as well as the official regulations and instructions of the Minister for State Security. According to its task, the MfS bears the main responsibility for combating hostile activity.

The nature and directions of hostile activity necessitate the consistent exploitation of the available instruments in socialist society to secure power, with a central position assigned to the application of socialist criminal and criminal procedure law, in conjunction with all other political, state, legal, and societal means, as well as political-operative forces, means, and methods, utilizing their specific potentials in a differentiated manner.

Hostile Agents

Persons who, on behalf of a foreign power, its institutions or representatives, or for a secret service or foreign organizations and their helpers, act subversively against other states, especially the socialist community of states, using conspiratorial, criminal intelligence means and methods. Even within their own imperialist power system, hostile entities employ agents, including informants, provocateurs, and undercover agents.

Hostile Attitude

A particularly pronounced and consolidated form of negative attitude towards the socialist state and social order and its ideological foundation, Marxism-Leninism. Hostile attitudes can lead to actions that openly or covertly aim to disrupt, halt, or reverse the development of the socialist state and social order as a whole or in individual areas. Actions based on hostile attitudes usually meet the criteria of socialist criminal law. Therefore, people with hostile attitudes must be identified in a timely manner in political-operative work (→ Attitude Analysis). The transition from hostile attitudes to hostile actions must be preventively countered with appropriate measures. People who engage in anti-state activities due to hostile attitudes must be consistently and purposefully addressed in operational work.

Hostile Group; Extraction of Persons

An operational method for recruiting informal collaborators, applied in dealing with hostile groups in operational processes. This method is characterized by the following aspects of the person to be extracted:

- A member of a hostile group,

- Suspected or strongly suspected of committing crimes, especially state crimes,
- Typically holds a hostile attitude, leading to criminal actions,
- After recruitment, is directly and significantly exposed to the political-ideological and other influences of the hostile group.

The goal of extraction is to infiltrate the conspiracy of the hostile group and gather information and evidence about planned, prepared, attempted, or executed hostile actions, as well as their means and methods. It also aims to find points of connection for paralyzing and restricting hostile actions or dissolving the hostile group.

Extraction is particularly necessary and should be considered when there are crimes of high social danger present or expected, requiring urgent clarification, or when the prospects of introducing an IM are low. For individuals with a strongly entrenched politically-ideological hostile mindset, extraction is often not possible or only very difficult. Extraction requires thorough and precise preparation, including:

Analyzing the operational process to determine the extent and intensity of the crimes, the evidence gathered, the group structure and atmosphere, and points of contact for covert contact, recruitment, and collaboration, especially → compromising material,

- Further investigation and review of individuals selected for extraction,
- Selecting the person who can achieve the greatest political-operational effectiveness and possesses the necessary prerequisites for covert, honest, and reliable collaboration with the MfS.

Effective methods for carrying out extraction include:

- Covertly bringing the individual in for questioning followed by recruitment,
- Recruitment under an appropriate operational cover for the actual reason for recruitment.

Sometimes, extraction is also achieved through long-term contact aimed at initially politically-ideologically winning back the candidate and gradually involving them in operational work.

Identification Features

The term for the reflected characteristics of the objects to be identified, used for analytical and comparative examination in the process of criminalistic identification. Depending on the different types of identification objects, these can be features of a person's appearance, dactyloscopic or writing features, voice and language features, features of the morphological structure of an object causing traces, and more. In principle, only the essential identification features are needed to solve the identification task in a specific case.

These are mainly those that are relatively unchangeable (stable), detectable (recognizable), and comparable over a certain period. Usually, a complex of identification features (feature combination) is used when examining the question of identity.

Identification, Criminalistic

A method based on Marxist-Leninist epistemology that contributes to a rational approach in information gathering, the investigation of objective truth, and the maintenance of objectivity, scientificity, and legality in investigation and evidence presentation. It finds broad application in various processes of political-operative work. The specific task of identification is to establish and prove the real conformity, i.e., the identity of operationally interesting or criminalistically relevant persons and objects with those already under review or still to be sought, investigated, or searched for.

Thus, identification essentially involves recognizing an object under review as the sought object and providing irrefutable proof that, for example, a specific person is the cause of traces, the author of writing, a speaker, a passport holder, etc., that the observation object is actually the operationally interesting person, or that the suspect is an employee of an imperialist intelligence service, that the confiscated weapon was used as a crime weapon, or that the found tool was used as a crime tool. It finds its main application under the conditions of the political-operative work of the MfS both within the framework of the → Expertise as well as in → Passport control (identity check in cross-border traffic), in operational → Observation, in operational → Manhunt, and in comparison and compression work.

The most important sub-areas of identification are → person identification and → Object identification.

Ideological Base

A person in the DDR who, due to their hostile-negative ideological position and professional, social, and other standing and opportunities, is built up and used by the enemy to increase the effectiveness of political-ideological diversion. Ideological bases adopt, develop, and write hostile ideological platforms, concepts, and other anti-socialist works and disseminate them in their areas of influence, partly misusing legal possibilities. Ideological bases maintain or seek connections with hostile organizations, organs, institutions, and forces in the operational area.

Image of the enemy, Chekist

The Chekist image of the enemy encompasses the entirety of knowledge and ideas about the nature and laws of imperialism, its subversive plans and goals against socialism, the forms of subversive activities and their attack directions, the hostile centers, organizations, and forces, the enemy's countermeasures, and the means and methods of hostile actions. It also includes the evaluations, feelings, and convictions based on this knowledge in the fight against the enemy. This image of the enemy is a specific manifestation of the scientific image of the enemy of the working class, based on the Marxist-

Leninist analysis of the class struggle, shaped by experiences and insights gained in the conspiratorial struggle against the subversive enemy. It is an inherent part of the ideology and moral value system and a significant characteristic of the Chekist personality.

In the process of political-ideological education of operative and unofficial collaborators, the comprehensive, individual, and methodologically versatile transmission and inculcation of the image of the enemy is constantly gaining importance. Concrete and reliable insights about the enemy and the deep feelings of hatred, disgust, aversion, and relentlessness towards the enemy based on them are extraordinarily important prerequisites for the successful fight against the enemy.

The more precisely and impressively the corresponding insights about the enemy are conveyed with their emotional weight in class-based education, the more the ability to recognize, investigate, and prevent hostile attacks in time, as well as the willingness and motives for actively combating the enemy, increase. One-sidedness, absolutizations, weakening, or distortions of the image of the enemy must not be allowed in political-operative work, as they can lead to wrong decisions and incorrect reactions.

Imagination

The specifically human process and ability to create new mental images from the images of reality conveyed by perceptions through their transformation and combination. With the help of imagination, humans can "form a picture" of things never previously perceived, anticipate future events and phenomena, and thus comprehend reality more deeply. In political-operative work, creative imagination is necessary, as developing variants, creating operative combinations, building legends, planning complex operative measures, and uncovering enemy plans and intentions require high imagination and strong visualization ability and, on the other hand, demand precise knowledge of reality in the respective area. Fantasizing, as an excessive imagination losing itself in forming increasingly unrealistic ideas and illusions and disregarding the real connections of practical struggle, leads to unrealistic speculations and gross errors in planning operative processes.

Imperialist Human Rights Demagoguery

A key component of the political-ideological struggle, where the politicians and ideologists of the imperialist bourgeoisie use the dilution, distortion, and falsification of human rights issues as a means to:

- Globally discriminate against socialism and interfere in its internal affairs,
- Apply pressure and coercion,
- Inspire, organize, and support hostile-negative forces as an anti-socialist ideological, personnel, and organizational base within socialist society,
- Disrupt and misuse the détente process,
- Conceal the nature of imperialist power structures.

Through human rights demagoguery, the opponent launches massive attacks on the power structures, state, democracy, freedom, and law within socialism. The plans of the opponents primarily aim to disintegrate, paralyze, and destroy socialist society "from within" by misleading its population, creating artificial conflicts, inspiring and organizing → political underground activities in the form of a "human and civil rights movement," organizing anti-state human trafficking, and making illegal requests to relocate to capitalist countries, as well as conducting anti-state propaganda.

Human rights demagoguery has a distinctly subversive character within the → political-ideological subversion and psychological warfare of the enemy. It is simultaneously a strategically and long-term planned component of the official government policy of the imperialist powers, a basis for the subversive activities of numerous hostile organizations, and combined with hostile activities of imperialism in foreign policy, military and arms policy, foreign trade policy, the acceleration of material war preparations, political and economic boycotts, and disruptive actions.

The offensive, preventive, and damage-preventive fight of the MfS against human rights demagoguery is of great and growing importance. As part of their enemy image, our staff and IMs must therefore have precise knowledge of the role of human rights demagoguery in the class struggle.

Imperialist Intelligence Services

Organs of the state power apparatus in imperialist countries. They are involved in realizing the class goals and interests of the monopoly bourgeoisie, maintaining and expanding imperialist power and exploitation relationships. They are instruments of rule for the monopoly bourgeoisie. Their class nature is determined by the deeply reactionary, aggressive, and expansionist nature of the monopoly bourgeoisie itself. Historically, imperialist intelligence services evolved from traditional repression organs (police, army) and the foreign policy apparatus of the bourgeois state into independent components of the modern imperialist power mechanism.

Their specific role in realizing the class goals of the monopoly bourgeoisie compared to other state organs arises from:

- Their assigned functions,
- The corresponding special circumstances of their political-legal and organizational classification within the mechanism of class dictatorship,
- The application and deployment of special intelligence forces, means, and methods, and

- The predominantly secret manner of their activities.

Thus, intelligence services in imperialist states are indispensable instruments for politically dominant circles to conceive and realize reactionary, aggressive imperialist domestic and foreign policies. Under the conditions of the growing economic, political, military, and ideological strength of real socialism on the one hand and the deepening general crisis of capitalism on the other, intelligence services gain increasing importance in implementing long-term diverse measures aimed at destabilizing socialist states to bring about counterrevolutionary changes. At the same time, proponents of confrontational policies increasingly use intelligence services to stir tensions worldwide and directly prepare military confrontations. Therefore, they receive special personnel, financial, and material support from imperialist governments. The powers and areas of responsibility of intelligence services are continuously expanded, and the control possibilities of bourgeois-democratic institutions over intelligence services are limited or de facto liquidated.

Consistent with their class nature, the following functions of imperialist intelligence services are recognizable (main directions of their activities):

1. Fight against real existing socialism through the use of the entire intelligence apparatus and comprehensive support for all imperialist attempts to realize aggressive counterrevolutionary objectives in socialist countries.
2. Active and comprehensive participation in the political protection of the exploitation order by deploying intelligence-specific forces, means, and methods to suppress, monitor, and control the revolutionary workers' movement and other anti-imperialist and democratic opposition forces in imperialist states.
3. Subversive struggle against the national liberation movement, especially against national liberated states of socialist

development and against peoples fighting for their liberation in Asia, Africa, and Latin America.

Moreover, intelligence services play an essential role in securing monopolistic special interests in the inter-imperialist power struggle of their states and in settling inter-factional disputes among the ruling circles of their countries. Different power groups try to secure the greatest possible influence in the intelligence services, especially in their leaderships. Currently, this influence is particularly exerted by the forces of the military-industrial complex. Intelligence services are important components of the military-industrial complex in the main imperialist countries. Therefore, the realization of their functions is particularly shaped by the aggressive and reactionary special interests of these power groups in imperialism.

Contrary to all attempts to portray them as purely "information-gathering" organs, intelligence services, with their entire apparatus, actively participate in the fight against the main revolutionary streams. Their main thrust is directed → regardless of location → particularly against real socialism, its state community, foreign representations, forces, and any activities supporting other revolutionary and anti-imperialist movements.

Classified based on their specific tasks into "reconnaissance" or so-called foreign and "counterintelligence" or so-called domestic, as well as technical reconnaissance and surveillance services, intelligence services are among the main organizers and main actors of subversive activities across the board. Especially through the deployment of agents and full-time employees, by exploiting legal opportunities in the "target countries" (diplomatic representations, accredited correspondents, journalists, commercial establishments, travel, transit, and tourist traffic), and through personnel infiltration of "key positions" within their power sphere, intelligence services realize their interrelated functions. Information gathering through espionage (against other states) and surveillance (within their states and occupied territories) holds a key position in the subversive activities of intelligence services. It serves both the decision-making processes of political leadership bodies and the realization of various other subversive activities by the intelligence services themselves or a multitude of frequently intelligence-directed other institutions and forces within the imperialist system of subversive activities. Intelligence services inspire and carry out illegal activities, such as organizing and inspiring "internal opposition" and underground political activities, politically-ideologically undermining, disrupting the continuous economic development in socialist states and national liberated states of socialist development, up to large-scale intelligence "operations" and other dangerous provocations that could severely endanger world peace.

The generally unrestricted ties of intelligence services to the highest leadership bodies of the executive and the granted powers enable extensive involvement of the potentials of various other state and non-state organs, organizations, and institutions of the imperialist domination system to camouflage and enhance the effectiveness of their subversive activities. To increase the effectiveness of subversive attacks, intelligence services also increasingly use the results of the latest scientific and technological developments. This goal especially in → attacks against real socialism is also served by intensified efforts for centralization, coordination, and cooperation at national and international levels. However, rivalries, competitive relationships, and mutual "control," driven by special interests, between intelligence services at the national level and between intelligence services of different states, are not excluded.

Imperialist Intelligence Services; Working Method

The manner of mobilizing and deploying all those forces, means, and methods deemed suitable to realize the functions of intelligence services. The working method is characterized by disregarding human dignity (and all its humanistic and ethical values), misusing modern scientific and technological knowledge, neglecting domestic legal norms, and violating universally accepted rules of international law.

Key components of the working method include:

- Working with recruited informers and agents for monitoring, undermining, unsettling, paralyzing, and destroying progressive or alternative social organizations and groups, as well as gathering espionage information,
- Personnel infiltration of official state and private institutions, companies, and other positions within their power sphere for internal intelligence control, surveillance, manipulation, and organizing subversive attacks externally,
- Misusing international, inter-state, and other agreements and arrangements and the legal opportunities arising from them, the activities of diplomatic representations and accredited journalists, and travel, visitor, and tourist traffic,
- Applying scientific and technological means and methods for imperialist domination security, qualifying espionage activities, and liquidating political opponents,
- Deploying special forces to conduct terrorist and other counter-revolutionary actions.

The working method of intelligence services possesses relatively high stability. Its development and modification are influenced by the international class struggle situation, the working method and effectiveness of intelligence services, the activities of socialist security organs, the political-moral state, and vigilance of the population. The increasing complexity in deploying means and methods, particularly the growing intertwining of using special covert and legal means and methods, is significant. The specific working method of imperialist intelligence services is influenced by the findings from analyzing political, economic, military, security-political, and other conditions in the target country, their own possibilities, subjectively different experiences of intelligence employees, and the specific target of subversive attacks.

The working method is characterized by the means, methods, and principles of seeking, reconnaissance, and recruiting spies, their training, instruction, and verification, the deployment of agencies to gather espionage information, and maintaining connections between intelligence headquarters and agents.

Imperialist Mass Media

A collective term for the imperialist press, radio, television, and associated institutions. The mass media have developed into an indispensable component of the imperialist rule system alongside traditional instruments of power. In fulfilling their class-bound educational, informational, and entertainment functions, they significantly shape the worldview and enemy image, views, behavioral norms, and values of broad sections of the population in capitalist countries. In the interest of the monopoly bourgeoisie, they contribute to anchoring the ruling ideology as the dominant ideology in the mass consciousness. As the ideological struggle intensifies, the importance of the imperialist mass media grows. The new possibilities resulting from scientific and technological progress are abused by them. In the strategic concept of political-ideological diversion, imperialist radio and television stations and their network of far-reaching transmitters play a central role as the most modern and fastest mass media. Imperialist ideology and lifestyle are transported across national borders day and night through these mass media in attractive, seemingly neutral packaging. The differentiated program design aims to reach as broad a population as possible in socialist states. In line with the main attack directions of political-ideological diversion, individual population groups are to be targeted and inspired to hostile actions. As instruments of aggressive imperialist foreign policy, the mass media prepare the mental soil for enemy activities by interfering in the internal affairs of socialist states, spreading lies, disinformation, half-truths, falsifications, and slanders. Such activities contradict international law norms and significantly hinder the normalization of interstate relations. Similarly, the activities of monopolistically controlled mass media are directed against the other two revolutionary main forces of the present. Together with these, the socialist states advocate that mass media contribute in their reporting "to strengthening peace, understanding between peoples, and the intellectual enrichment of the human personality."

Incident Investigation; Preparedness

The constant and active assurance of a swift and offensive deployment, including appropriate political-operative actions by the operational forces of each operational service unit, oriented towards the possible occurrence of politically operative significant → incidents, to guarantee the immediate and comprehensive clarification and investigation of politically operative incidents while simultaneously restricting and averting serious consequences.

Preparedness requires:

- Developing an operational situation assessment-based identification of incident-prone areas/objects,
- Qualifying operational staff regarding their immediate deployment and operational activity in clarifying and investigating politically operative incidents and decisively countering the dangers and consequences arising from such incidents,
- Developing the capabilities of IM and GMS for immediate and independent action upon the occurrence of incidents,
- Ensuring early operational cooperation oriented towards incident investigation with other organs,

- Providing and ensuring the functionality of a quickly deployable technical basic equipment.

Incitement

Influencing an usually undefined group of persons to engage in hostile-negative actions, such as work stoppages, threats and use of violence, gatherings, demonstrative-provocative behavior, interference, etc. Actual corresponding actions by the incited persons do not need to occur.

Incitement can — when necessary objective and subjective conditions are met — reach the quality of state-hostile agitation according to § 106 StGB or a criminal offense of obstructing state or social activities according to § 214 StGB and represent other differentiated legal violations.

Incitement differs from instigation according to § 22 para. 2 no. 1 StGB. Instigation, as the intentional determination of another to commit a criminal offense actually committed by the instigated person, always occurs against specific perpetrators and refers to a specifically determined criminal offense.

Inciting Slogan, Anti-State

A written or oral, usually brief, visually or acoustically quickly perceivable and memorable statement aimed at public effectiveness, suitable, and intended to attack or incite against the constitutional foundations of the socialist state and social order of the DDR according to § 106 StGB.

Inciting slogans are usually placed in written form on a carrier material in a way that is well visible to a broad audience.

Individual Interests

The concentration of a person's intentions and participation in a specific area of interest to recognize and master it accurately.

Individual interests are, therefore, a significant regulator for attention to a matter and simultaneously a motive to engage with it. Individual interests are relatively stable orientations towards specific, subjectively experienced values. Interests, like needs and ideals, act as motivation for action. In the process of recruiting candidates for IM and informal cooperation with IM and secret employees, they form essential components of their motives.

Researching interests in operational activities must first focus on capturing their structure, showing whether a specific interest dominates or is subordinate to others. For example, an interest can become a very stable attitude towards a subject area that is appreciated, preferred over others, defended against attacks, promoted, and recommended to others. Conversely, an interest can act as a tendency when it occasionally arises but is entirely overshadowed by other interests at other times.

Additionally, the scope or breadth of interest areas, the degree of interest development, and the intensity with which they are pursued should be considered when utilizing or influencing the interest situation. These interest characteristics provide clues about versatility or one-sidedness of interests as a prerequisite for intellectual breadth and harmonious education or explanations for intellectual narrowness and disharmonious education. They also allow conclusions about fragmentation, superficiality, one-sided narrowness, and the persistence or fleetingness of interests.

Infiltrator

A person who, through the use of conspiratorial means and methods, moves people or items unnoticed across the state border to another country.

Infiltrators include:

- Members of imperialist intelligence services maintaining connections to their agents for continued communication and smuggling activities.
- Individuals employed by criminal human trafficking gangs or in connection with hostile entities and persons to smuggle people and items.
- Private individuals acting independently to smuggle people or items across the state border.

Influence

Purposeful impact on people, their opinions, attitudes, and behaviors. Influence occurs, depending on the underlying class interest, as persuasion (under socialist societal conditions) or as → manipulation (under the conditions of the imperialist ruling system). Influence in operational activities aims at developing behavior and performance traits of the personality that promote and enable the fulfillment of the political-operational tasks of the MfS in various areas. This requires clarity on ideological questions of working with people, detailed knowledge of personality qualities, understanding the dialectical relationship between external influences and internal conditions, and mastering pedagogical-psychological laws of personality development and education. Depending on the content and pursued class interest, influence usually takes the form of persuasion, instruction, positive/negative sanctioning, coaxing, suggestion, and manipulation.

Information Flow

The information flow encompasses the transmission of information through specifically determined paths and within a certain period to the employees, service units, management levels, leading party, and state officials, and partners in operational cooperation who need it to solve their tasks. The information flow is initiated by:

- requests for information in the form of orders to IM, reporting requirements, assignment requests, and other forms of requests,
- assessment of the importance of information for the leader, certain operational service units, and other recipients.

The information flow must correspond to the recipient's information needs, conveyed through operational reports and other individual pieces of information, as well as feedback information, and must comply with the requirements of conspiracy, secrecy, and security. Information flows between service units are regulated based on official regulations and instructions or through coordination guidelines. Within the service units, the information flow is specified by instruction.

Information Gathering

The information gathering encompasses the constant and systematic acquisition of operationally significant information by the Unofficial Collaborator (IM) and Company Employees for Security (GMS), other operational forces, means, and methods, as well as by utilizing the possibilities of other social forces to meet the information need.

Information gathering is an indispensable prerequisite for realizing political-operative tasks and, therefore, an essential part of all operational work processes.

Prerequisites for information gathering are primarily:

- task-oriented determination, specification, and transmission of the information need, especially based on analytical work during the realization of operational processes,
- creation, qualification, and specific deployment of operational forces, means, and methods,
- well-functioning information flows.

Additionally, prerequisites for information gathering include:

- thorough evaluation of party and state leadership resolutions and documents,
- comradely official cooperation with leading cadres and specialists in areas to be secured,
- the exchange of information with party organs, social organizations, and institutions, etc.

In a broader sense, information is obtained through new insights during the analytical processing of existing information.

Instructor Connection

A basic type of conspiratorial connection system between imperialist intelligence services and their agencies in a target country of their hostile activities. It primarily serves for training and instruction, handing over written instructions, necessary intelligence tools, material compensations, and receiving interesting information and items through personal connections. The instructor connection can include the personal courier connection.

Intelligence Contacting

A phase in the process of approaching target individuals by employees or → agents of → imperialist intelligence services to prepare and carry out their recruitment for subversive activities or → intelligence extraction. Contacting in the DDR is done by resident agents acting as DDR citizens, incoming agents from non-socialist foreign countries and West Berlin, and disguised employees of intelligence services posing as members of diplomatic and other missions of imperialist states abusing their legal positions in the DDR. In non-socialist foreign countries, contacting is mainly conducted by intelligence service employees.

Intelligence Evaluation of Failures

A specific form of analysis and evaluation of causes, favorable conditions, and consequences of not achieving intelligence objectives. The careful evaluation of so-called intelligence failures, i.e., primarily the arrest of agents by socialist security organs, the discovery of other intelligence activities, and the infiltration of their agent networks and offices by socialist scouts, is carried out by the intelligence services according to certain criteria.

Depending on the type of failure, they include:

- The search for personal, psychological behavioral, and security-related failures in the recruitment and control of the respective agent,
- The reconstruction and evaluation of the recognition, processing, and arrest of detained agents by the socialist security organs, and
- The initiation of measures deemed necessary to ensure the security of the affected intelligence services and associated facilities or further sources, based on the incident or the assumed or verifiable disclosure of the real possible knowledge of captured spies, identified scouts, etc.

The evaluation serves primarily to prevent a recurrence and increase the security of future intelligence activities and the forces, means, and methods employed.

Intelligence Misuse

The extensive organized use of state organs, non-state organizations, institutions, and forces, as well as state and non-state relationships, by imperialist intelligence services for initiating, organizing, and carrying out espionage and other subversive activities against the revolutionary mainstreams of the present, particularly against socialist states, to achieve counter-revolutionary aggressive objectives.

The intelligence services widely exploit the official connections and influence opportunities arising from the structure of bourgeois states, existing personal entanglements of a private nature, and especially the significant infiltration of all areas of social life by agents.

The various concrete manifestations include the intelligence misuse of diplomatic representations and their personnel with gross disregard for international law (misuse of → diplomatic rights), the intelligence misuse of commercial facilities (→ economic disruptive activities), and the intelligence misuse of individuals, particularly in → entry and transit traffic.

Intelligence Recognition Meeting

A necessary meeting between an intelligence officer or → instructor/courier and agents who have not been personally known until then, such as after a long period of inactivity. Recognition meetings occur at pre-agreed locations and times, using specific → recognition signs or → code words for mutual identification. The term recognition meeting became particularly known through CIA activities.

Interference

Violation of international law by one or more states intervening in the internal affairs of another state. The policy and activities of interference pursued by imperialist states, especially the BRD (Federal Republic of Germany), against the DDR (German Democratic Republic) express the aggressive and expansionist nature of imperialism and are part of the imperialist state policy, including measures aimed at the long-term counterrevolutionary elimination of the power structures in the DDR. This interference policy is closely linked with the subversive activities of imperialist intelligence services, centers of political-ideological diversion, and other enemy centers and groups. The imperialist policy and activities of interference are further characterized by their opposition to détente and the unscrupulous misuse of the European treaty system. They are associated with the promotion of imperialist human rights demagoguery and an intensified, though modified, revanchism by the BRD towards the DDR, primarily shown by maintaining the legally invalid position of "keeping the German question open."

From the experiences and insights into the nature of enemy interference and considering the tasks of its active combat, it is necessary to categorize interference as a violation of international law into three fundamentally politically-operative significant types:

1. The exertion of unacceptable political, ideological, or economic pressure by the BRD to impair the exercise of sovereign rights of the DDR (unacceptable pressure exertion).
2. The usurpation of sovereign rights of the DDR by the BRD (usurpation of sovereignty).
3. The incitement of DDR citizens by the BRD to engage in subversive and other illegal activities against the constitutional order of the DDR (subversive interference/incitement).

The implementation of the imperialist interference policy always includes attempts to impair and violate the state sovereignty, territorial integrity, and political independence of the socialist state, as well as to undermine the political decision-making freedom of state organs and citizens. Specifically, the interference actions emanating from the BRD against the DDR aim to undermine the exercise of the DDR's sovereign rights regarding the state border and its security, citizenship, legal, judicial, and penal sovereignty, the shaping of the DDR's relations with other states, and the incitement of DDR citizens to engage in anti-state and other illegal activities.

The BRD and other imperialist states increasingly strive to implement interference actions against socialist states through the subversive misuse of treaties and agreements and the misuse of the rights granted to diplomats, correspondents, corporate and bank representatives, etc. By the coordinated cooperation of imperialist intelligence services and other state organs with non-state institutions, organizations, and groups (issuing orders, instructing, financing), attempts are made to conceal the interference practices of imperialist states to evade political and legal responsibility.

General democratic international law prohibits interference. Interference actions are violations of international law. The illegality of interference derives from the universally binding and mandatory principle of non-interference in matters within the domestic jurisdiction of states, enshrined in Article 2, Section 7 of the UN Charter, defined in the UN Declaration on Principles of 24 October 1970, elaborated in bilateral and multilateral treaties such as the Helsinki Final Act (Principle VI), and concretized in the Treaty on the Basis of Relations between the DDR and the BRD of 21 December 1972 (Article 6). Interference actions simultaneously violate other mandatory principles and norms of international law by imperialist states (e.g., sovereignty principle). Only states (subjects of international law) or state organs, including intelligence services, judicial bodies, and state institutions acting or failing to act in violation of international law, can be subjects of interference, for whose consequences the state is responsible to the affected state (object) (international legal responsibility).

Given the changing conditions, the MfS has increasingly important tasks in preventing, uncovering, and combating illegal interference actions, including timely clarification of enemy plans, intentions, and measures. High-quality standards are required for the precise documentation of incontrovertible and politically exploitable facts and evidence of interference actions. This is a crucial basis for their active rejection and combat with political, politically-diplomatic, legal, and politically-operative offensive measures to effectively support the domestic, foreign, and security policies of the party and state leadership of the DDR.

Internal Security of the Ministry for State Security (MfS)

The unrestricted political-operational readiness, combat effectiveness, and reliability of the MfS as a specific organ of the dictatorship of the proletariat. It must be continuously ensured through the daily work process and duty-conscious behavior in the leisure area. This requires continuous comprehensive preventive political-operational security of the organs, employees, family members, unofficial collaborators, former members, official, covert, and residential objects, as well as the communication and other connections of the MfS against attempts of infiltration, espionage, disorientation, disorganization, and insecurity, as well as other subversive attacks, particularly by imperialist intelligence services and other hostile institutions, groups, and individuals. Internal security is thus both a component and an indispensable prerequisite for successful political-operational task fulfillment.

To ensure it at all times requires constant influence from official leaders, the basic organizations of the party, and the FDJ to strengthen and deepen the political-ideological and political-moral clarity and firmness of each member and the collectives.

This is the most important prerequisite for timely recognition of attacks against the MfS and their preventive prevention. It is necessary to draw and implement continuous conclusions for their education and training to steadfast communists with pronounced Chekist qualities, abilities, and knowledge according to the specific political-operational and class struggle conditions and the development level of the personnel.

Particularly important are:

1. Implementing the far-reaching, significant resolutions of the SED party congresses in unity with the resolutions of the CPSU party congresses in political-ideological educational work and work with the personnel, qualifying the education of members based on the program and statutes of our party and the personnel documents of the MfS, especially by further shaping the socialist way of life in the workplace and leisure area, as an important basis for the preventive prevention of attacks by imperialist intelligence services against MfS members.
2. By strengthening the preservation of traditions, conveying knowledge about the history, role, and significance of the MfS, as well as specific Chekist role models, and developing pride in being a member of the MfS, an organ of the dictatorship of the proletariat, revered by the people and hated by the enemy.
3. Further shaping or developing such attitudes among active and future MfS personnel that express the view that service in the MfS is not just a common, albeit well-paid, profession, but a calling by the party of the working class that must be fulfilled daily.
4. Further developing the enemy image of MfS members generally (regarding the aggression, misanthropy, and danger of imperialism and its intelligence services) and specifically according to the activity and tasks of the individual member by imparting specific knowledge about the enemy's goals, intentions, and methods.
5. Strengthening the education in maintaining secrecy, confidentiality, and revolutionary vigilance, developing behavioral norms in the event of actual or suspected attacks by imperialist intelligence services on MfS members and their family members, and enabling them to perceive their responsibility for increasing their security and the security of the MfS in both service and family and leisure areas. The unchangeable goal must be to make every individual member of the MfS politically-

ideologically and politically-morally invulnerable to the enemy, thus ensuring the absolute internal security of the MfS.

Interrogation of Suspects

1. Criminal procedural examination measure according to § 95 Abs. 2 StPO, applied in the politically-operational work of the MfS as a method to obtain politically-operationally and possibly legally significant information and effectively support politically-operational measures, such as the destabilization and unsettling of hostile and other negative groups. It serves, depending on the specific political-operational objective, particularly to:

Examine the suspicion of a criminal offense and, in connection with this, determine and secure → official evidence based on available unofficial evidence.

- Clarify further politically-operationally and legally significant actions of the suspect and other persons as well as politically-operationally interesting connections, persons, and groups, including their inspirers, backers, and connections.

Elicit reactions from the suspect and other persons to destabilize or unsettle hostile and other negative groups and support → evidence collection when checking initial clues, developing operational → source material, and processing operational → personal controls and → operational cases.

The interrogation of suspects according to § 95 Abs. 2 StPO may only be carried out by employees of the Investigation Line. The investigation departments, in close cooperation with the responsible other political-operational service units, must ensure that:

- The intended political-operational goals are likely to be achieved.

- Politically negative and harmful consequences are excluded.
- The reactions of the suspect after the interrogation are controlled.
- The legal and investigative tactical requirements are met.

2. The interrogation of a suspect can also take place within the framework of bringing them in to clarify a situation based on § 12 Abs. 2, 2nd paragraph of the Law on the Tasks and Powers of the German People's Police (VP Law). It is bound by the legal requirements of the VP Law. This possibility is primarily used in politically-operational work when the necessity of interrogating a suspect arises from an unforeseen situation requiring immediate action. The same politically-operational requirements as for an interrogation of the suspect according to § 95 Abs. 2 StPO generally apply to the conduct of the interrogation.

The interrogation within the framework of bringing in to clarify a situation based on § 12 Abs. 2, 2nd paragraph in conjunction with § 20 Abs. 2 VP Law can be carried out by all MfS employees. The responsible investigation department must be informed immediately.

Investigation Planning

A part of investigative work.

An intellectual-creative process in which, based on the matter to be investigated and with consistent consideration of the criminal and criminal procedural requirements as well as the valid orders and instructions of the MfS, the goals, focuses, means, and methods of investigative work in an → investigation procedure or in political-operational → incident investigation are determined and continuously refined.

The main function of investigation planning is to ensure effective and targeted investigation management with the aim of comprehensively and impartially establishing objective truth. It serves the consistent enforcement and strict adherence to socialist legality as well as ensuring high political and political-operational effectiveness of investigative work.

Investigation planning is primarily embodied in the written investigation plan, which represents the basic operations plan for handling an investigation procedure or investigating a politically and operationally significant incident and serves as an effective control and guidance instrument for investigative work.

The investigation plan, in accordance with the task of investigation planning, particularly includes the following components:

- The political, political-operational, and legal objectives of the investigation,
- Investigation versions,
- Assessment and evaluation of evidence,
- The basic line of investigation tactics,
- Investigation focuses and complexes,
- Determinations for political-operational evaluation activities.

Based on the investigation plan, plans for individual investigation actions, such as interrogation plans, action plans, tasks for experts, etc., are developed.

Investigative Work

Political-operational work of the investigation departments of the MfS, whose specifics are determined by exercising the powers as a state investigative body.

Guided by orders and instructions from the Minister for State Security, investigative work is essentially characterized by the same features as political-operational work. However, it is also characterized as a state activity regulated by criminal procedure within the framework of a criminal process, requiring official measures to implement socialist legality; the necessity and possibility of conducting criminal procedural investigation and security measures in the investigation process and the criminal procedural review stage (e.g., questioning, interrogating suspects and witnesses, criminal procedural coercive measures); its associated international effectiveness.

Integrated into the overall tasks of the MfS, investigative work aims to optimally contribute, according to the requirements and possibilities of each investigation process or respective → incident investigation, to support the offensive policy of the party and state leadership, including the offensive repulsion of imperialist interference policy and activities and other violations of international law, the preventive prevention, detection, and combating of subversive attacks, plans, and intentions of the enemy and other politically and operationally significant actions, further increasing state authority, consistently implementing socialist legality, and further strengthening citizens' trust in the socialist state power, especially the MfS, objective comprehensive and thorough clarification of each committed crime, its causes and conditions, and the offender's personality as a prerequisite for holding each guilty party consistently and differentiatedly criminally accountable while not persecuting any innocent person, further perfecting the cooperation of the Chekist brother organs in the fight against the enemy and in the clarification and combating of crime overall, targeted support of the political-operational work of other MfS lines and service units, particularly within the clarification process "Who is who?", for strengthening the operational base and further qualifying the handling of operational processes, effective and timely damage-prevention measures, and ensuring high security and order in all areas of social life.

To achieve these fundamental tasks of investigative work, there must always be reliable assurance of objectivity, scientific approach, and partisanship in handling the means and methods of investigative work as a prerequisite for truthful investigation results.

Investigative work builds on political-operational work results from other lines and service units of the MfS and is closely connected with their political-operational work processes in many ways. The requirements of evidence gathering guide the entire political-operational work, as the political and operational benefit of any legal application can only be secured on the basis of significant and irrefutable evidence. Investigation results must be verified operationally, and conversely, political-operational work results can be confirmed or refuted through investigative work. Only within these close interrelationships can investigative work achieve high quality and effectiveness.

The fulfillment of the tasks of investigative work also requires political-operational cooperation with other state organs and institutions, particularly with protection, security, and justice organs. Depending on the tasks and powers of these organs, the cooperation primarily serves to realize legal obligations related to the implementation of criminal procedural measures (e.g., issuance of an arrest warrant by the competent court, prosecutor's order for search and seizure); conveyance of experiences and insights of the MfS in recognizing hostile activities and other politically and operationally significant contexts; securing and continuously developing information relationships; exploiting specific means, methods, and possibilities (e.g., the powers of customs administration in cross-border traffic).

Under current political-operational conditions, investigative work is organizationally divided into two closely intertwined sub-areas:

- The processing of investigation processes based on initiated investigation procedures,

- The investigation of politically and operationally significant incidents based on the criminal procedural review process.

Investigative Work; Means and Methods

Political-operational and criminal procedural measures as well as methodological instruments to achieve the fundamental tasks of investigative work.

These include, in particular:

Conducting → questioning of individuals and interrogations of suspects and witnesses,

- Mastering interrogation tactics,
- Securing evidence and records,
- Applying forensic means and methods,

Obtaining → expert opinions,

→ Investigation planning,

Realizing the requirements of → evidence gathering,

- Verifying investigation results through political-operational measures,
- Objective documentation of investigation results,
- Qualified evaluation and information activities,
- Cooperation with the brother organs of other socialist states as well as with other service units in the MfS,
- Participation in the realization of political-operational tasks of other service units in the MfS,
- Cooperation with the prosecutor's office, court, and social forces as well as with other state investigative organs,
- Preparing and conducting public relations measures (e.g., journalistic measures, preparing the court trial).

Justified Risk Action

An action taken by a person to achieve a societal advantage or avert a societal disadvantage, where failure cannot be completely ruled out. Individuals may face situations that demand risky decisions and behaviors. This risk can be considered justified if:

- The action was taken to achieve a societal advantage or avert a societal disadvantage,
- A responsible examination of all circumstances determining the action and its impact was conducted, and the possible safety precautions for the success of the action under the given objective and subjective conditions were taken,
- The intended societal success was highly probable,
- The intended societal advantage significantly outweighs the possible societal disadvantage, or the potential damage is less than the damage to be averted.

See also § 169 StGB

Latency of Hostile Activity

In political-operative language, the term for the entirety of intended, planned, and committed state crimes, politically-operative significant general criminal offenses, and other hostile actions that the security organs are not yet aware of.

To uncover the latency of hostile activity, it is necessary to prove through targeted political-operative and investigative work that certain occurrences or actions are politically-operative and criminally significant. State crimes may have remained unknown due to their sophisticated execution methods and may be hidden behind politically-operative significant general criminal offenses,

- other legal violations,
- legally unrecognized phenomena/occurrences.

Politically-operative significant general criminal offenses not yet uncovered may also be hidden behind other legally significant or legally unrecognized phenomena/occurrences.

Other hostile actions, activities, and intentions of the enemy may initially remain unknown to the security organs due to their new attack directions, means, and methods.

The effective uncovering and limitation of the latency of hostile activity is an essential component of the overall state and societal crime prevention and combating efforts. Prerequisites for uncovering the latency of hostile activity include precise knowledge of the security requirements arising from the social development processes in the DDR, the integration processes within the socialist community of states, and the international class struggle between socialism and imperialism, the analysis of completed → operational and investigation processes concerning possible expected hostile activity, and continuous qualified operational and investigative activity to clarify politically-operative significant actions in close cooperation with state and economic leadership organs, economic units, social organizations, and citizens.

Leading Question

An inadmissible question in the interrogation or questioning of individuals in criminal proceedings or other politically operative processes. Leading questions suggest specific answers from the outset and can thus distort the statements of the interviewee/questionee.

Leading questions are often answerable only with "yes" or "no" and do not lead to a detailed, verifiable statement of the interviewee. They are generally unsuitable for obtaining true statements about the matter to be clarified.

In exceptional cases, with secure knowledge about the subject of the question, leading questions can be used as a tactical means to induce the willingness to testify.

Leisure area

The leisure area is the part of social life that encompasses the relationships and activities outside the work process, including the related social, cultural, municipal, and other institutions. In the leisure area, a significant part of the fundamental social, cultural, social, and physical activities and needs of people are realized or satisfied. The leisure area has a significant influence on the development of personality and overall behavior.

Ensuring order, discipline, and security in the leisure area, as well as primarily the preventive prevention, uncovering, and combating all attempts by class enemies to become active in the leisure area and misuse it for their subversive goals, is a key task of political-operative activity. Analyzing the leisure area and political-operative activity within it are essential prerequisites for assessing people, influencing people, specifically for investigating persons of operative interest and preventive security, and solving other political-operative tasks.

Lie Detector

A term for apparatuses suitable for recording and documenting physiological reactions occurring in the human body, which are mass-produced.

Various types of devices are used in the USA as part of the state security program by trained personnel of US intelligence agencies, state police, and security officers of corporations and detective agencies.

The approach known as the polygraph procedure is based on scientific findings from medicine, psychology, and interrogation tactics. The simultaneous registration of several reaction sequences, triggered by carefully selected questions and corresponding psychological attunement of the test person, can yield characteristic criteria that allow conclusions about suppressed emotional reactions.

Line Principle

A principle of the organizational structure of the MfS, according to which operational service units at the central and district levels have specific responsibility for securing certain social areas, combating specific enemy attack directions, or realizing specific operational work processes (e.g., investigation, observation).

The responsibility of the operational service units on the line includes contributing significantly to achieving the uniformity of operational actions in all operational service units of the MfS according to their responsibility for securing specific social areas, combating specific enemy attack directions, or realizing specific operational work processes. To fulfill this special responsibility, they primarily use → planning orientation and methods of → coordination. The line principle is implemented in the organizational structure of the MfS in unity with the → principle of individual leadership, the → focal principle, and the → territorial principle.

Long-Term Conceptions

A planning document for anticipating the orientation of political-operative work processes and leadership activities toward long-term existing and emerging security requirements. They serve long-term → planning and are developed to:

- Secure selected societal areas, objects, processes, territories, and groups of people,
- Develop and qualify specific operative processes and meet further long-term political-operative work requirements.

Long-term conceptions, based on the assessment of the → political-operative situation, contain determinations about:

- Fundamental objectives for securing societal areas, objects, processes, territories, or
- Significant political-operative goals and tasks directed towards the fundamental objective and the stages for their realization, particularly for developing, processing, and completing operative cases and developing and conducting operative person controls,

Directions for the use and further development of operative forces and means, especially unofficial collaborators (IM), including the development and use of the operative → basis for work in and after the → operational area,

- Organization of cooperation with other service units and political-operative collaboration with other organs and further necessary leadership tasks.

They often include relevant determinations for cadre work and material-technical and financial support. The necessity, subject, and timing of the development and the duration of validity are decided, unless otherwise directed, by the leader responsible for their realization and confirmation of the conceptions.

Loyalty

A personality trait expressing great consistency in the individual's behavior towards social phenomena, values, and norms. In the Chekist sense, a specific quality of the MfS members' relationship to the working class, their party, and the socialist state; it is the lasting commitment to the party and government's policy, based on a firm class standpoint, political, ideological, theoretical clarity, and emotional connection. Loyalty as a specific form of attitudes is inseparable from socially valuable character traits such as trust and devotion, readiness for commitment and sacrifice, courage and discipline, and unconditional combativeness and steadfastness.

Main Task of the MfS

The general requirement for the work of the MfS arising from the → security needs of socialist society and the → security policy of the party. This general requirement consists of ensuring the state → security of the DDR against all attacks by internal and external enemies.

The main task of the MfS includes:

1. Investigating the enemy's plans and intentions,
2. Ensuring internal state security,
3. Organizing work in and after the operational area,
4. Cooperating with state organs, economic institutions, and social organizations to prevent favorable conditions and harmful actions preventively.

All these tasks of the MfS are closely related. To realize them, a system of political-operative intelligence and defense organs, operative-technical, and other service units has emerged, characterized by high specialization, creative self-responsibility in implementing the party's decisions and the minister's orders, effective political-operative performance, and goal-oriented cooperation between the MfS's line-specific and territorial service units.

Overall, fulfilling the main task of the MfS must lead to work results suitable for providing the party with timely strategic and tactical information about the enemy, investigating, disrupting, and combating the enemy in their bases in the operational area, preventing hostile machinations against the DDR, uncovering internal enemies, ensuring the security of the DDR under all conditions, and preventing damage and harmful actions through prevention, higher vigilance, discipline, and order.

Mass Psychological State, Operationally Significant

Psychological relationships and interactions in larger spontaneous gatherings of people, usually in a particular state of tension, often mistakenly referred to as mass psychosis. Forms can include mass panics during war events and disasters, mass actions by religious fanatics, ecstasy-induced music fans, or others manipulated and incited through psychological means in capitalist countries, mass hysteria among racists, National Socialists, counter-revolutionaries, anarchists, and similar groups. Mass psychological states are a reflection of the deformation of people by the exploitative order and their mental manipulation by the ruling class. These states can also affect politically unstable individuals or anti-socialist elements in the DDR. For example, they were evident in isolated negative gatherings and mass riots of youths.

Factors to consider in negative gatherings with a mass psychological state include:

- The rapid spread of negative moods and passions in gatherings of people with negative attitudes,
- The imitation of aggressive, oppositional, or criminal behaviors by agitators, initiators, and leaders, by other individuals who are susceptible to such calls,
- The passive toleration of excesses, rowdiness, etc., by a larger number of spectators or vocal followers.

Political-operational measures must account for the peculiarities of mass situations and their mass psychological state. This requires:

- Timely recognition of signs of mass gatherings and preventive measures to prevent them,
- The exposure and isolation of agitators, initiators, leaders, and differentiation between active participants, followers, and spectators in the use of police measures.

Meeting

A confidential, covert meeting between the IM-leading employee and the IM to systematically realize the goals and tasks of covert collaboration and maintain a secure connection with the IM. It must be conducted with the strictest observance of high vigilance and secrecy in working with the IM, protecting the IM and ensuring their conspiracy and security, while respecting the individuality of the IM and their relationships with the leading employee.

The meeting holds a special position in collaboration with the IM, as it primarily ensures concrete personal and subject-related task assignments, instruction, and reporting, as well as the associated education, empowerment, and verification of the IM. This results in high requirements for preparing, conducting, and evaluating the meeting.

Meeting Conduct

The direct course of the confidential, covert meeting between IM-leading employees and the IM. The focus of the meeting conduct is on concrete personal and subject-related task assignments, instruction, and reporting, as well as the associated education, empowerment, and verification of the IM.

The following principles must be observed during the meeting conduct:

- The IM-leading employees must be role models to the IM, maintain a clear class standpoint, and involve the IM in discussions on significant political and political-operational issues.
- When making assessments and decisions, the IM's attitudes and their connections to the MfS must be considered. For personal problems of the IM, possible help must be discussed without making unfulfillable promises.

- The IM must be convinced of the demands placed on them. Objections and concerns of the IM must be addressed factually but with appropriate consequence.
- The IM must recognize that no outside person knows about their collaboration with the MfS and their information is evaluated without jeopardizing their conspiracy. Meetings are to be conducted in covert apartments or covert objects.

Meetings at other locations are an exception and require confirmation.

Members of the MfS

All female or male employees of the MfS who have been hired and certified according to the official regulations and have a rank. The members of the MfS perform their service in the employment relationship of a professional soldier or in the employment relationship of a temporary soldier.

Members of the MfS; Recruitment

The conviction necessary in the process of recruiting new members into the service of the MfS to develop the candidate's readiness to join the MfS service, considering all requirements and the personal consequences arising from them. It is only permissible after the search and selection and sufficient intelligence when the suitability of recruitment candidates, their previous performance, especially their positive political attitude and reliability, have been verified and when there are no fundamental doubts about their suitability.

Recruitment is realized through targeted personal discussions, in which the corresponding readiness is achieved and developed, possibly over a longer period, based on existing solid political-ideological attitudes and character-moral qualities. For → perspective cadres, it is realized based on the already existing readiness for unofficial cooperation.

Members of the MfS; Requirement Profile

The entirety of general Chekist qualities and behaviors that serve as a general assessment standard and as the goal of Chekist education and qualification for all members of the MfS. The Requirement Profile is derived from the objective requirements of the struggle against the enemy and is defined in the party resolutions, official regulations, and instructions of the MfS, especially in the fundamental documents of cadre work. It includes:

- firm connection with the working class, loyalty to it and its Marxist-Leninist party and the worker-peasant state, firm friendship with the Soviet people and the other socialist brother countries, high socialist consciousness, and high personal combat and readiness for action,
- the willingness and ability to maintain conspiracy and secrecy and to ensure the internal security of the MfS,
- sufficient life experience, positive character-moral development, and qualities,
- education or prerequisites corresponding to the requirements of Chekist work,
- the ability to successfully carry out politically-operative/professional activities,
- good health constitution, physical and psychological performance, and good general resilience. Based on the Chekist Requirement Profile, concrete requirements must be derived from the respective tasks and especially defined in the functional and qualification characteristics.

Microdot

A photographic reproduction technique that creates an image at a reduction scale of approximately 1:50 to 1:300. Imperialist intelligence services use microdots to transmit espionage information within their communication systems. The transport of microdots is carried out via a connection path determined by the intelligence service (postal or personal instructor-courier connection). The particular advantage of the microdot technique lies primarily in its extremely small size, which allows for a variety of concealment options. They are hidden in various objects, predominantly in postal items, or covertly embedded into texts of letters or printed materials, making them undetectable without optical aids. Generally, a magnification of about 150 times is sufficient to decipher a microdot. This can be done using a microscope or a microfiche reader, as available in all modern libraries or documentation and information facilities. The recipient of the information must have possession of such equipment or have access to it. The production of microdots is relatively straightforward with current technology but requires knowledge and experience in document photography and lab techniques, as well as access to the necessary equipment and chemicals.

Military Inspection (MI)

A group of members from the U.S., British, and French armed forces stationed in West Berlin, with a frequently changing composition of uncertain size, conducting so-called inspection tours in the capital of the DDR, Berlin, based on specific, coordinated assignments with the imperialist intelligence services. This occurs under the pretense of "control rights," for which there has been no foundation since the abolition of Berlin's former four-power status (1948). By maintaining their presence in the capital of the DDR, the Western powers attempt to politically demonstrate their adherence to the alleged ongoing four-power status of the DDR's capital, which contradicts the actual legal situation of the DDR's capital as an integral part of the DDR.

Notwithstanding the legal positions of the USSR and the DDR, which do not obligate the DDR to grant a special status to such military personnel, the DDR considers a de facto practiced approach in relation to the MI, stemming from the joint administration of

Berlin by the four powers in the post-war period, in the interest of détente. Accordingly, the DDR currently permits the entry and temporary stay of Western military personnel, including MI members, in the capital of the DDR, which includes the obligation to respect the DDR's legal order.

The MI's subversive actions in the capital of the DDR focus on:

- The immediate reconnaissance of the purpose, nature, and security of military facilities, installations, and movements, the offices of the Soviet Armed Forces Group in Germany (GSSD), Soviet government representatives, Soviet residential areas, the NVA, the DDR border troops, and other armed bodies, particularly the MfS,
- Determining the combat and deployment technology of the GSSD and the DDR's armed bodies, as well as the dislocation of their forces and resources,
- Systematically locating covert facilities and installations of Soviet intelligence and counterintelligence, as well as the MfS of the DDR,
- Identifying the purpose, nature, and security of party and government facilities, protocol routes and facilities of diplomatic representations, as well as transportation, supply, and communication facilities, and the facilities and installations of economically important enterprises.

In connection with these subversive activities, further legal violations are committed by MI members to expand their action capabilities, evade operational control, and avoid measures by the protective and security organs of the DDR and the GSSD due to these legal violations.

The task of the MfS, in cooperation with other protective and security organs, is to monitor the movements of the MI in the capital of the DDR, to timely identify, document, and prevent their subversive and other unlawful actions, and to further restrict the illegal use of their action capabilities.

Misuse of Art and Culture

Efforts by internal and external enemies to misuse the socialist society's art and culture sector for conducting political underground activities and other various forms of enemy activity, especially for spreading anti-socialist views, theories, platforms, concepts, and other subversive content. The enemy tries to misuse or repurpose the influence opportunities of these sectors on socialist consciousness formation by establishing ideological → bases and unconstitutional alliances among artists and cultural workers and mass media employees.

Motivation for Operational Actions

An individual psychological phenomenon, such as a need, interest, feeling, ideal, attitude, or conviction, that initiates and directs an individual operational action toward a goal. Current feelings, a suddenly arising interest, or a thought can act as motivation, just as existing psychological traits of the operational forces can.

Typically, several motivations underlie an operational action, collectively referred to as the motivation for the action. To assess the operational action, it is necessary to clarify the underlying motivations, as the outward appearance of an action does not provide a clear characterization of its essence.

New motivations must be generated for every action taken by operational forces.

Negative Attitude

A personality trait expressing a relatively consolidated, rejecting, destructive, pessimistic, also reactionary personal relationship to social progress in general or to phenomena, development trends, and laws of developed socialist society in particular. Since negative attitudes can negatively affect the socialist state and social order, they must be identified in → operationally significant persons in a timely manner and assessed differently according to the operational objective (→ Attitude Analysis), and reduced through appropriate measures of → Attitude Formation.

Negative Grouping

Loose associations of mostly young people with relatively similar lifestyles and moral views deviating from the socialist way of life, and unclear, unsteady, sometimes already negative political-ideological attitudes.

Negative groupings constantly pose dangers due to their spontaneous behavior or reaction to state measures, potentially disrupting public order and security, and quickly transitioning to anti-state actions, such as terror and violent acts against the state border of the DDR.

Negative groupings are unstable in their composition, with no unified goals or tasks guiding their actions. Members of negative groupings meet based on situations, time, or habit at street corners, cinemas, restaurants, parks, but also in clubhouses and other gathering points.

Nonviolent Uprising

Hostile concept and practice aimed at gradually undermining state power and seizing power positions in individual socialist countries through intensified psychological warfare, particularly → politically-ideological diversion, and by using other hostile and subversive means and methods. The nonviolent uprising is a model in the planning and organization of the counterrevolution. It is a variant of adapting imperialist warfare to the changed class power relations in the world. It is the enemy's attempt to carry out the counterrevolution in such a way that the socialist states cannot provide solidarity aid to the attacked country.

The strategy and tactics of the nonviolent uprising are to be gradually realized under the significant leadership and involvement of the imperialist secret services and in close cooperation with other hostile centers.

The imperialist models of the nonviolent uprising include specific steps and measures for building counterrevolutionary bases, infiltrating key positions in the state, economy, culture, mass media, organizations, and armed forces, disrupting the state's functionality, and collaborating with internal and external counterrevolutionary and imperialist forces. In preparation (→ political underground activity; → internal opposition) of the nonviolent uprising, the enemy concentrates all available means and methods on the politically-ideological influence of selected persons or groups, particularly those who influence public opinion in their countries and can actively affect the masses. The models of the nonviolent uprising show the alignment of the strategy and tactics of this concept with the concept of covert warfare and recognize the possibility of combination.

Object Security

The totality of preventive political-operative, military-operative, and operative-technical measures to ensure the security of an object important for societal and economic development as well as for the protection and security of the German Democratic Republic, the processes taking place in it, and its environmental relationships.

The main objective of object security is to prevent the penetration of persons acting on behalf of imperialist intelligence services or other hostile organizations, institutions, and forces, to effectively combat direct attacks against the object to be secured, to constantly ensure order and security in the object, and to avoid damage.

Object security is carried out within the framework of a → security concept.

Objectivity of Political-Operative Work

A political-operative way of thinking and behaving that is inseparably linked with socialist partisanship and results from it, oriented towards the societal laws, operative requirements, contexts, processes, and facts independent of consciousness, explicitly rejecting subjective positions, and ensuring and enforcing socialist legality.

Objectivity as a way of thinking and behaving in political-operative work is expressed primarily in the objectivity of analytical work and information activities, in the application of objective and thus optimal operative methods and means, in the objectivity of informal and criminal-procedural evidence, and in the conscious and explicit ensuring and enforcing of socialist legality.

The principle of objectivity and the unity of communist partisanship, strict objectivity, and consistent scientificity must always be consciously enforced at a higher level in the process of further qualifying the political-operative work of the MfS.

Observation Ability

A complex of personality traits of operational forces required for successfully conducting observations in general operational activities (observation of the witness during interrogation, observation of the suspect by the IM during conversation) and specifically for → operational observation. Observation ability consists of intentional and systematic perceptual performances aimed at tracking the course of an operationally significant event or the changes occurring in the observation object. It primarily includes optical and acoustic perception abilities, quick, logical thinking, clear judgment and memory, conscious attention, and concentration, which gain different weights under the influence of specific observation activities and form the specific structure of observation ability. Observation ability can be acquired through intensive learning, practice, and training.

Odor Differentiation

A method for identifying persons based on empirically secured knowledge that every person has a unique and specific odor. Unintentionally, a person transfers parts of their odor to their environment through direct contact when touching objects or walking.

Odor traces are secured using sterile dust cloths, tongs, and tweezers, avoiding odor contamination at the → event sites, crime tools, and other trace-carrying objects. The comparison materials (odor preserves) needed for differentiation are either directly taken from body parts of suspected persons or covertly secured from their worn clothing items or touched objects.

Secured odor traces and odor preserves are stored and transported in sterile, airtight sealed Weck jars. In exceptional cases, odor-trace-carrying objects can be temporarily secured and transported in clean plastic bags.

The result of odor differentiation cannot be used as evidence in criminal proceedings. In conjunction with other operative and criminalistic measures, it helps narrow down the circle of suspects to identify the perpetrator.

Securing odor traces should generally be done by trained specialists. Odor differentiation is conducted by specially trained dog handlers (differentiation dog handlers) with trained dogs (differentiation dogs).

Offender's Personality

The entirety of the social and ideological relationships and positions, as well as the psychological and physical characteristics of an → offender in their development and inner connection to the crime. The development of the offender's personality is characterized by the active engagement of the person with societal and natural conditions of their environment, taking into account the primacy of societal conditions, involving a complex interaction between these external factors and the internal conditions in the form of the psychological and physical characteristics of the offender. In this process, under the influence of imperialist ideology, hostile or politically negative attitudes towards certain areas of social life emerge, which are a crucial basis for the decision to commit crimes. The personality of offenders who commit → state crime is significantly shaped by anti-state attitudes. This personality stands in an antagonistic contradiction to the constitutional foundations of the socialist state and social order, where their individual anti-state attitude must be differentiated according to its ideological content, extent, and degree of consolidation. Anti-state attitudes must be distinguished from the many other negative political attitudes that, while also contrary to the moral norms of the working class, do not have a hostile character. Such negative political attitudes are typically found in offenders who commit politically and operationally significant crimes of general criminality.

The offender's personality also influences the → manner of committing and the impacts of the crime. It is also a crucial basis for determining individual criminal responsibility and establishing appropriate measures of criminal responsibility. The scope and limits of clarifying the offender's personality are generally determined by the violated criminal offense of the StGB - Special Part - considering the corresponding norms from the General Part of the StGB, the political and operational objectives of processing the respective operational case or investigation procedure, and the requirements for interrogation tactics.

The clarification of the offender's personality is particularly related to:

- the personality development in its various areas of life and stages,
- the social behavior in individual areas of life (profession, leisure, public, social work),

- connections to persons and institutions, their development, intensity, and quality,
- the material and social living conditions,
- the political and ideological attitudes, the ideological influences reflected in them, and the mental maturity,
- the specific goals and motives of the crime.

The substantive criteria for clarifying the offender's personality are also significant for the → incident investigation, the implementation of → operational person controls, and the type of conclusion of → operational processes. Furthermore, by clarifying the offender's personality, it is possible to recognize the causes/conditions favorable to the effectiveness of hostile influences and to draw conclusions for the prevention of crimes.

Operational Adaptability

Operationally significant characteristic of operational forces that enables them to consciously behave according to the operational task and the situational conditions. Operational Adaptability includes flexible reactions to facts, engaging with different people, and enduring the cover story. The behavior controlled by Operational Adaptability can, in one case, align with the views, attitudes, and values of the operational forces, and in another case, contradict these inner attitudes. Operational Adaptability is characterized by the ability to realize behavior according to the operational goal despite the contradiction between inner attitudes and the required operational task.

However, operational forces must be particularly motivated for this. Operational Adaptability can be developed through knowledge transfer and practical training.

Operational Base

The totality of persons in the own territory on whom the MfS relies to fulfill its tasks.

The possibility of cooperation or collaboration with these persons arises mainly from the advantages of socialist society, from the responsible exercise of the rights and duties enshrined in the DDR constitution by the citizens of our country, and their resulting willingness to participate in fulfilling important tasks to secure societal development and protect the socialist order.

The core of the operational base consists of persons active as IM, GMS, and officers on special assignments. Furthermore, the MfS relies on many forces working in state institutions and organizations and other suitable persons. Depending on the development of the socialist society and the effectiveness and influence of the MfS and its members, the operational base is constantly evolving. Utilizing this trend, uncovering and realizing new potentials of the operational base is an important leadership task, whose solution unlocks significant reserves for the fulfillment of the MfS's tasks.

Operational Combination

An operative method that represents a complex of interdependent, complementary, and coordinated measures aimed at compelling certain persons to reactions that enable or create favorable conditions for solving operative tasks while maintaining the secrecy of the intentions, measures, forces, means, and methods of the MfS. To offensively trigger reactions while maintaining secrecy or to ensure that certain reactions do not occur, suitable operative → legends are necessary in the operative combination.

The main component of the operative combination is the covert use of reliable, operatively experienced, and suitable unofficial collaborators (IM) for solving tasks. Combinations are largely based on real, existing circumstances and conditions. The prerequisite for developing combinations is the availability of sufficient and qualified information about the facts or target person. Developing combinations requires a logical approach and necessitates:

- Developing the objective of the operative combination and analyzing the initial situation,
- Creating the rough draft and refining the operative combination,
- Developing a plan for the intended operative combination and determining and preparing for the use of IM and other operative forces, means, and methods.

The combination is carried out based on a specific written plan. The success of a combination largely depends on strict, unified leadership to promptly resolve any complications that may arise. The combination is particularly applicable:

For using IM in processing operational cases, e.g., → introducing and inducting IM, disengaging, or verifying these IM,

- For creating legally usable evidence, e.g., through the use of criminalistic means and methods to obtain comparison material,

For preventing crimes, e.g., through the use of → decomposition, disinformation of hostile forces, or operative-technical means,

- For realizing complicated recruitments, e.g., to create compromising material or ensure the presence or absence of persons,
- For realizing covert inducements and searches.

Operational Decomposition

An operational method of the MfS for effectively combating subversive activities, especially in case processing. Through various politically operative activities, influence is exerted on hostile-negative individuals, particularly on their hostile-negative attitudes and beliefs, in such a way that these are shaken or gradually changed, or contradictions and differences between hostile-negative forces are triggered, exploited, or intensified.

The goal of decomposition is the fragmentation, paralysis, disorganization, and isolation of hostile-negative forces to prevent, significantly limit, or completely stop hostile-negative actions and their effects or to enable a differentiated political-ideological → recovery. Decomposition measures are both an immediate component of the processing of → operational cases and preventive activities outside of case processing to prevent hostile consolidations. The main forces conducting decomposition are the IM. Decomposition requires operationally significant information and evidence about planned, prepared, and conducted hostile activities as well as appropriate points of connection for the effective initiation of decomposition measures.

Decomposition must be carried out based on a thorough analysis of the operational situation and precise determination of the specific objective. The implementation of decomposition must be uniformly and strictly managed, and its results documented. The political sensitivity of decomposition imposes high demands on maintaining conspiracy.

Operational Immediate Measures

Measures that must be initiated immediately after becoming aware of a → political-operative incident. The responsible operational service unit in whose jurisdiction the political-operative incident occurred is always responsible for the implementation of the immediate measures. The immediate measures aim to immediately establish the necessary conditions for the successful execution of the political-operative → incident investigation. These measures usually consist of a complex of operational actions, including:

- Developing a maximum amount of initial information,

- Ensuring the securing of evidence through securing the incident site and preserving traces and other evidence,
- Averting or preventing dangers, other negative impacts, and the occurrence of further incidents, and
- Initiating the political-operative incident investigation as an operational process.

To ensure high effectiveness, all suitable operational forces, means, and methods must be used in the complex. The content, form, and nature of the individual immediate measures depend on the character of the political-operative incidents and the political-operative situation in the area of the incident.

Operational Investigation

General: A method for obtaining information in political-operational work through covert conversations conducted by operational forces with individuals likely to possess the required knowledge and used as → informants, as well as through database queries or evaluation of written documents. Investigations are conducted unofficially or officially, depending on the requirements.

1. Specific: Covert collection of operationally significant information through covert conversations by IM investigators with informants and covert use of databases. Investigations are initiated based on confirmed assignment requests and serve primarily to provide a thorough assessment of individuals in operational processes, such as handling operational cases, operational person checks, security checks, clarification/review of IM candidates, etc. Investigations are conducted in work and leisure areas.

Qualitative criteria for valuable investigation results include covert processing, high informational value, and objectivity. The results of the investigation are documented in an → investigation report.

Operational Liaison System

The entirety of forces, means, and methods used by the MfS to establish and maintain a secure and always functional connection with the IM. The connection is an important prerequisite for systematic, trustful, conspiratorial work with the IM, for the realization of political-operational tasks under the most diverse political-operational conditions, and for a rapid and secure flow of information between the IM and the MfS.

The liaison system is particularly exposed to enemy attacks. Therefore, it must always correspond to the requirements of conspiracy and must not offer the enemy and other persons any opportunities to recognize IM or to penetrate the IM stock.

Components of the liaison system, also referred to as types of liaison, include:

- Meetings in conspiratorial apartments or conspiratorial objects,
- Telephone connection (direct or via cover telephone),
- Postal connection (usually through cover address),
- One- or two-way radio connection,

Use of rendezvous points, deposit points, and → Dead Letter Boxes (DLBs),

- Application of signal signs/signal points.

To ensure the necessary stability, security, and mobility of the connection, several types of liaison are usually combined. It must be ensured that:

- Individual arrangements are made with each IM, especially for the legend of the meetings and for behavior during telephone connections, which must be documented in the IM files and updated if necessary,
- The IM are prepared and able to implement the agreed arrangements practically,

- The liaison system is subjected to constant differentiated testing and verification.

In operational parlance, the term "liaison system" is also used.

Operational Marking

An operational-technical method of covertly marking persons and objects using chemical substances with reliably detectable properties (marking agents). It serves to obtain information about operationally relevant actions of these persons or about the relationships between persons and objects where such actions can occur. The chemical substances suitable for marking allow:

- Marking complete series of objects to identify imitated objects due to the absence of marking (e.g., permissions for border crossings, seals for securing closures on vehicles or other objects).
- Safely identifying marked objects and materials from a multitude of identical or similar but unmarked objects and materials (e.g., marked documents, letters, banknotes, fuels, and weapons).
- Determining through preventive marking of endangered objects whether, when, and where these objects were (temporarily) removed from their place of storage (e.g., securing classified documents, weapons, and other objects against unauthorized and unnoticed removal from the office).
- Detecting the use of marked objects and materials for anti-state actions (e.g., marked writing instruments or papers for the production of inflammatory letters, additional copies, or transcripts).
- Recognizing changes in marked objects, their position, condition, or set value (e.g., opening of closures, changes in constant settings of aggregates, or unauthorized opening of envelopes).
- Determining if and which persons or objects have come into contact with a marked object (e.g., by unauthorized entry into a pre-marked room or touching marked objects).

Essential prerequisites for implementing marking measures include:

- Repeated execution of similar enemy actions against a specific object,
- Extensive clarification of the means and methods used by the enemy for this purpose,
- Identification of a suspicious person or a limited circle of suspects through informal tips and operational determinations,
- Or the presence of justified suspicions about expected specific anti-state activities.

The success of a marking depends on knowledgeable and thorough preparation, which must be realized in close cooperation between the commissioning service unit and the operational-technical specialists. Organizing the informal work to obtain the necessary initial information, bringing marked objects to the suspect, monitoring the marking and the suspect circle, etc., is fundamentally important for the comprehensive legend and conspiracy of the operational-technical measure. The complex use of marking agents and other operational-technical means and methods can significantly increase the effectiveness of the marking in many cases.

Operational Method

A system of principles, rules, recommendations, or directives for solving specific political-operational tasks. The method outlines how operational forces and resources can be deployed covertly, offensively, and with high effectiveness to achieve defined goals.

Operational methods arise from, or are the result of, the generalization of operational experiences, operational and scientific insights. The application and further development of the method in political-operational work are based on the laws, conditions, and requirements of the struggle against the enemy, the applicable legal provisions, and the official regulations and directives within the MfS. When applying a method, the local, temporal, and other conditions (→ operational tactics) must be considered.

Examples of operational methods include:

- Extracting individuals from hostile groups,
- Introducing IMs into the processing of operational processes,
- Removing IMs from the processing of operational processes,
- Decomposition,
- Operational cover story,
- Operational combination,
- Operational game.

Operational People Skills

The individually varying ability of → operational forces to understand the psychological characteristics of individuals and predict their behaviors. This skill develops primarily through personal experiences in interacting or working with people, such as during → recruitment and → collaboration with IMs, in handling cases, in the work of investigators, in → operational investigations, operational observations, and in leadership activities.

Judgments based on people skills are often intuitive and usually not explicitly formulated, directly influencing behavior and decision-making toward others. People skills facilitate interpreting behaviors, quickly orienting oneself with a relationship partner, recognizing and considering individual peculiarities, and applying operational → cover stories, among other things.

Depending on the nature of personal experiences, judgments based on people skills can be more or less accurate. Sources of error that limit the reliability of such judgments include overestimating first impressions, letting prejudices and subjective standards influence decisions, making false generalizations, and so on.

Therefore, people skills should be developed further through the acquisition of knowledge and skills for the methodical and conscious assessment and evaluation of individuals.

Operational Situation

A collective term for:

1. Information about facts that are evaluated as operationally significant and for which politically operative measures are necessary to determine further details, connections, causes, conditions, or backgrounds, or to prevent damage in time, eliminate favorable conditions for crimes, etc. Examples of operational situations include findings on:
   - Actions that resemble the methods of enemy activity,
   - Connections and contacts of persons in the operational area,
   - Hostile-negative or other attitudes directed against socialist development, negative personality traits (e.g., careerism or greed),
   - Events/incidents. In general, operational situations should be recorded according to official regulations and instructions in the MfS's storage.
2. Objective, value-free representation of facts known in politically operative work, which reflects the currently known knowledge about operationally significant events/incidents completely or partially. These can be results of incident investigations, security checks, processing of operational personal controls or operational processes, processing of investigation procedures, and other operational processes.

Operational Tactics

The theory and practice of deploying operational forces, means, and methods to achieve political and operational tasks under consideration of location, time, and conditions to reach the desired goals rationally, effectively, and safely. Tactics are primarily derived from the insights, experiences, and conclusions of political and operational work in the fight against the enemy. The determination and establishment of tactics are essential components of planning, preparing, and executing operational measures. This requires in particular:

- deriving from the goals of the operational measures,
- analyzing the plans, intentions, measures, means, and methods of the enemy for subversive activities,
- knowledge of the abilities, skills, and experiences of the operational forces as well as knowledge of the deployable operational means,
- observing and complying with legal regulations, official provisions, and instructions as well as the rules of conspiracy and secrecy,
- selecting suitable operational methods, especially for offensive influence on persons/groups,
- a justifiable ratio of effort and benefit.

The tactical approach is often described in more detail in the operational methods or generalized in them for specific applications or purposes.

Operationally Significant Clues

The state of knowledge reached as a result of the politically-operative and legal assessment of information that hostile-negative actions and attitudes of persons or their misuse by the enemy may exist. Operationally Significant Clues often indicate the preparation or execution of hostile-negative actions or corresponding plans and intentions but do not yet constitute suspicion of a criminal offense. Operationally Significant Clues are prerequisites for initiating Operational Personal Control. Operationally Significant Clues can result from verified and usually already condensed information about

- actions (acts or omissions) that may be possible ways of engaging in hostile-negative activities,
- negative and rejecting attitudes towards socialist development or the policies of the party and state leadership, which persons express or spread,
- operationally significant contacts and connections between persons from the DDR and persons, institutions, or organizations from the operational area,
- further politically-operative personality traits that can be starting points for misuse by hostile-negative forces. The evaluation of information as Operationally Significant Clues is based on
- politically-operative knowledge and experience about plans, intentions, measures, methods of operation, and means and methods of hostile-negative forces,
- the politically-operative situation in the area of responsibility and current politically-operative requirements,
- already recognizable or expected damage or danger points for internal security,
- the applicable legal regulations in the DDR,
- official regulations, instructions, and orientations of the minister and related determinations,
- the security-political significance, activity, position, influence, and personality of the person concerned.

See also Operational Personal Control.

Operationally Significant Incident

A surprise occurrence of anti-state or general criminality or socially harmful actions, events, or incidents that must be clarified and investigated by the operational service units of the MfS. The decisive criteria for assessing the political-operational significance of an incident are:

- Indications of suspected enemy activity,

- The presence of significant damage or danger,
- A significant threat to internal or external security,
- Extensive negative effects on public sentiment.

These criteria must be differentiated and creatively used to assess an incident, considering the current political situation in the area of responsibility. Any incident assessed as politically operative significant must be promptly and comprehensively clarified and investigated through a political-operative → incident investigation.

Operationally Significant Mass Psychological Condition

Often mistakenly referred to as mass psychosis, this term describes psychological relationships and interactions in larger spontaneous gatherings of people, usually in a certain tension situation. Manifestations can include mass panics during war events and disasters, mass actions of religious fanatics, ecstasy-induced music fans or other psychologically manipulated "fans" in capitalist countries, mass hysteria among racists, National Socialists, counterrevolutionaries, anarchists, etc. Mass psychological conditions here are expressions of human deformation by the exploiter order and mental manipulation by the ruling class. Through various influences, these are also effective among politically unstable persons or anti-socialist elements in the DDR. They were evident, for example, in isolated negative gatherings and mass riots of youths.

Factors to consider in negative gatherings of people in a mass psychological condition include:

- The rapid spread of negative moods and passions among gatherings of people with negative attitudes,
- The imitation of aggressive opposition or criminal behaviors of agitators, initiators, and leaders by other active individuals on prepared ground,

- The passive toleration of excesses, rowdyism, etc., by a large number of spectators or loud followers.

Political-operational measures must take into account the peculiarities of mass situations and their mass psychological condition. This requires:

- Timely recognition of signs of mass gatherings and preventive measures to prevent them,
- Unmasking and isolating agitators, initiators, leaders, and differentiating between active participants, followers, and spectators when using police means.

Operative Forces

The totality of the officially and unofficially deployed staff to solve the political-operative tasks of the MfS. The operative forces include:

→ Members of the MfS

- in operative service,
- Officers on special assignment,

→ Unofficial Collaborators (IMs),

- Full-time IMs,
- Prospective Cadres (Prospective Cadres),

Social Employees for Security (→ Social Employees for Security).

Operative Forces; Behavioral Line

Orientation, guideline, or model for the necessary behavior of operative or IMs in solving a conspiratorial political-operative task. The behavioral line results from the character of the task, the objective of the assignment, the general circumstances for its realization, and the always unique political-operative situation. It must be aligned with the personality (especially the operative skills and experience) of the employee or IM/Social Employees for Security who should behave according to a given behavioral line. The behavioral line aims for a system of actions and reactions of the person that creates the impression of a consistent and non-contradictory behavior, thus serving the fulfillment of the assignment and ensuring compliance with conspiracy. Therefore, it must include:

- Specification of the necessary behavioral acts in relation to the situations and events that require them,
- Indications of the entirety of circumstances that can promote or hinder the realization of tasks,
- Variants for unforeseen events or circumstances (accident, encounter with acquaintances, identification, etc.),
- Orientations for the application of the evasion legend and its modification by unexpected circumstances.

→ Adaptability

Operative Person Control (OPK)

Operative process to clarify → operative significant clues. The political-operative objectives of OPK are:

Development of the → suspicion of committing crimes according to the first or second chapter of the criminal code - Special Part - or a crime of general criminality that has a high degree of societal danger and is closely related to state crimes or for whose elaboration the MfS is responsible (targeted development of → initial material for operative processes),

- Identifying persons with hostile-negative attitudes or operative significant connections and contacts, from whom hostile-negative actions can be expected under certain conditions and circumstances, and timely preventing or limiting their corresponding effectiveness,
- Preventive securing of persons who are or will be active in security-politically particularly significant positions or areas and

who, due to existing clues, are at risk of being misused by the enemy, and thus timely recognizing and effectively combating hostile attacks or hostile-negative actions by these persons.

In accordance with this objective, OPK is an essential part of clarifying the question "Who is who?". In OPK, all necessary preventive, damage-preventing measures, including those for timely recognizing and eliminating hostile-negative actions, promoting circumstances, and conditions, must be initiated and implemented. The results of OPK must be constantly analyzed and assessed to timely refine the control objectives and initiate the necessary political-operative measures or be able to conclude the OPK.

Operative Process (OV); Conclusion

Stage of handling operative processes in which, through the application of politically-operative effective and legally permissible (especially based on the criminal procedure code) measures, the proven crimes are to be suppressed as completely and finally as possible, further crimes are not to be allowed, and the preventive measures made possible by this are to be realized.

The objectives of the conclusion are in detail:

- To further prove and suppress the already recognized hostile activity or other crimes according to the established evidence,
- To eliminate their concrete causes, promoting conditions, and circumstances through influence on the responsible organs, enterprises, combines, and institutions as well as social organizations,
- To prevent further hostile-negative actions and initiate or increase measures to ensure safety and order,
- To maximize internal security in the area of responsibility and thus help to enforce the policies of the party and government as a whole.

The prerequisites for the conclusion, which must be checked and assessed throughout the handling of operative processes, are:

- The class struggle or political-operative situation makes the conclusion necessary or allows it,
- The political-operative objectives of process handling were realized with the required quality and to the necessary extent, especially through the proof of the urgent suspicion of a crime.

For the conclusion, a concentrated assessment of all process material must be carried out from political-operative, criminal law, and criminal procedure points of view, resulting in conclusions about the existence of the prerequisites, the specific objective of the conclusion, the most effective type of conclusion (or partial conclusion), the method of realization of the conclusion, and the evaluation of the results achieved with the operative process. Corresponding decisions must be proposed to the responsible leaders.

The types of conclusion according to official regulations and instructions are:

- Initiation of an investigation procedure with or without detention,
- Recruitment,
- Application of decomposition measures,
- Recruitment,
- Use of process material as compromising material against corporations, enterprises, institutions, state organs of the Federal Republic of Germany, other non-socialist states, or West Berlin,
- Initiation of specific measures against privileged persons,
- Transfer of material on general criminal offenses to other protection and security organs,
- Public evaluation or transfer of material to leading party and state officials, combined with proposals for preventive measures to ensure safety and order.

A → final report must be prepared for the conclusion.

Operative Process (OV); Introduction of IM

Operative method of the MfS to establish confidential relationships between the suspect and a qualified, verified, and suitable IM for the respective task in Operative Processes with the aim of obtaining operatively significant information and evidence through the confidential relationships about planned, prepared, or already conducted hostile-negative actions, the underlying motives, as well as means and methods of the suspects and their accomplices, and thus create prerequisites for the prevention, hindrance, or restriction of the hostile-negative actions.

The introduction requires bringing an IM closer to the suspect and expanding the contacts achieved until establishing confidential relationships between the suspect and the IM. It is applied when no suitable IMs are working on the suspect or when, despite already existing IMs, more IMs need to work directly on the suspect.

According to the status, circumstances, and conditions of processing an Operative Process and the already deployed IMs, the following principles of the introduction must be observed:

- The introduction must be carefully prepared already at the beginning of the processing of Operative Processes,
- The number of IMs to be introduced must always be determined depending on the specific political-operative requirements and conditions of processing the Operative Process,
- The introduction must be designed so that the initiative to establish, maintain, and deepen the relationships with the IM comes from the suspect,
- The introduction is only successful when concrete results for achieving the goals of the Operative Process could be obtained.

To prepare and conduct the introduction, the following is required:

- Precise definition of the political-operative tasks to be solved by the introduced IM according to the goal of the Operative Process,

- Development of a requirement profile for the introduced IM based on the defined political-operative task, analysis of the suspect's personality, and the circumstances and conditions of processing the Operative Process,
- Selection of a suitable and capable IM that largely meets the developed requirement profile,

Development of suitable operative → legends and → operative combinations to bring the IM into the suspect's view and encourage the suspect to establish and deepen contact,

- Preparation of the IM for their deployment,
- Responsible assignment and instruction according to the established operative-tactical approach for the introduction as well as careful reporting by the introduced IM.

Throughout the entire introduction, it must be conscientiously assessed what stage has been reached and to what extent the goal of the introduction has been achieved. Also, the → extraction of the introduced IMs must always be ensured. When processing hostile groups in Operative Processes, the necessity and possibility of → breaking out individuals from hostile groups must be examined simultaneously when deciding on the introduction.

Oral Incitement, Anti-State

An anti-state action punishable under § 106 StGB, carried out through direct verbal expression or using sound equipment such as loudspeakers, playback devices, etc., or by misusing telephone connections, aimed at attacking or inciting against the constitutional foundations of the socialist state and social order of the DDR.

Person Hideout

In connection with subversive activity, particularly state-hostile human trafficking (§ 105 StGB) and illegal border crossings (§ 213 StGB), hidden or created cavities in cars or other means of transport to accommodate persons for the purpose of their smuggling out of, into, or through the DDR or other socialist states. Person hideouts can be:

- Existing cavities in cars and other means of transport, such as trunks, wheel wells, suitable as person hideouts,
- Cavities created through structural modifications in cars and other means of transport, suitable as person hideouts,
- In the cargo of cars and other means of transport.

Person hideouts are primarily used by criminal → human trafficking gangs and individual smugglers but can also be used by intelligence services, other hostile organizations, and criminal gangs.

→ Shelter and Hideout Possibility

Person Identification

A subfield of criminalistic → identification that includes identifying suspicious and other operatively interesting individuals. These may include trace-causing individuals, anonymous or pseudonymous writers or speakers, fugitive lawbreakers, individuals living under false names, employees of imperialist intelligence services, objects of operative → observation or operative → search, or unknown dead. The primary methods of person identification are → dactyloscopy, → handwriting examination, phonetic examination (→ speaker identification), and person identification based on physical characteristics (→ personal description). Additionally, person identification may also involve blood group analysis, stomatological examinations, and specific forensic medical examinations of the human skeleton. The prerequisites for successful person identification include the availability of qualitatively and quantitatively suitable crime and other source materials in the form of papillary ridge traces, handwriting materials, voice recordings, personal descriptions, photographs, blood and saliva traces, hair, teeth marks, etc., as well as the procurement and evaluation of corresponding comparison material from suspicious or to be checked individuals.

Perspective Cadre

1. Recruitment candidates primarily prepared and tested for the political-operative service of the MfS. They are selected based on the general requirements for MfS members, initially used as IM or GMS, and after proving themselves, they are employed by the MfS.
2. Recruitment candidates selected according to the cadre or educational needs of the MfS among students of universities and colleges, used for political-operative work during their studies, and after proving themselves, employed by the MfS.

Working with perspective cadres is of great importance for ensuring the internal security of the MfS, particularly for recognizing and developing the suitability and reliability of new recruits. Intensive cooperation with perspective cadres is required, especially in their education and training to solve chekist tasks.

Planning of Political-Operative Work

The mental preparation and forward-looking decision-making about the specific political-operative goals, tasks, and measures in the respective area of responsibility, the deployment of operational forces and means, the formulation of corresponding accountable guidelines, including responsibility and deadlines for the realization of target and task assignments in the planning documents. Planning is an essential aspect of leadership activity. Its function is primarily to:

- Implement the principle of focus, especially through the development, determination, or refinement of political-operative focus areas and priorities and the specific approach to their political-operative security or processing,

- Lead the unified and coordinated actions of all service units to realize the overall task of the MfS under the respective conditions of the political-operative situation,
- Connect the solution of current tasks with the preparation for the solution of future tasks and ensure the necessary continuous development of political-operative work, especially the operational forces, means, and processes,
- Mobilize the creative initiative of all members of the MfS to realize ambitious goals, tasks, and measures.

The unified and coordinated actions of all service units are ensured in the planning process through plan guidelines and plan orientations, as well as by coordinating plan specifications and confirming plans by supervisors. The continuity, long-term character, and concreteness of planning are ensured, among other things, by the content-related connection of long-term planning, annual plans, operative plans, action plans, plans for the preparation and execution of operative actions and security operations, etc. Long-term planning determines fundamental, beyond one year, political-operative goals and tasks, the determination of the main directions of deployment and development of operational forces and means, and the essential realization stages and is a significant basis for annual planning. It is realized through long-term plan guidelines and plan orientations, long-term concepts, and long-term plans. The respective task determines the content design of the plans.

Fundamental planning principles for political-operative work are, in particular, the resolutions and documents of the party and state leadership, plan guidelines, plan orientations, and other service regulations and directives, existing long-term concepts, the assessment of the political-operative situation, and the results of coordination between service units of the MfS and other organs.

Political Underground Activity

One of the most dangerous manifestations of subversive activity.

It is inspired by the concentrated use of → political-ideological diversion and organized by hostile centers, organizations, and forces seeking, collecting, and merging hostile-negative forces to create a personnel base within the DDR.

These forces aim to fight against the DDR long-term, using covert means and methods to establish anti-socialist positions in socialist society, incite DDR citizens against socialism, activate hostile actions, and thereby initiate the process of counter-revolutionary changes to ultimately eliminate the power of workers and peasants.

Political underground activity poses a high societal danger. It targets the political, ideological, and economic foundations of socialist society as a whole, as well as the socialist legal order, and is punishable by law.

Political Underground Activity; Precursors

The entirety of negative political-ideological attitudes, anti-social, oppositional, and hostile-negative behaviors and actions that, in their practical-political consequences and development tendencies, have a real relationship to political underground activity and can transition into it.

The precursors of political underground activity include, in particular:

- Negative and hostile discussions over a long period in certain circles and groups that belong to the target groups of the enemy, where deficiencies, grievances, and development problems in socialism are constantly discussed without principles, questioning the fundamental issues of the party and government policies, adopting and spreading arguments used by the enemy in political-ideological diversion, and ongoing negative political

discussions based on anti-socialist literature not permitted in the DDR within such circles and groups.
- Writing and distributing politically and ideologically unclear writings that deviate from or distort Marxism-Leninism and the fundamental questions of party policy, especially when there is a suspicion that these are the beginnings of a hostile platform.
- Attempts by individuals to exploit and abuse legal opportunities, e.g., within the framework of the Cultural Association, Urania, or under the guise of religion, in discussion evenings, book readings, etc., to spread the enemy's ideology, exaggerate deficiencies, difficulties, and development problems in our society, extend criticism to fundamental issues of party and state leadership policies and our social development as a whole, and organize readings or exhibitions in private where negative literature or works of visual art are published or spread, especially if negative or hostile individuals are preferentially involved.
- The frequent occurrence of unlawful requests to relocate to the BRD and West Berlin in certain areas and territories, especially when these requests are predominantly politically motivated, provocative, and associated with threats, when the same hostile-negative arguments repeatedly occur, and the manner of justification suggests that the applicants cannot be the authors themselves but were inspired and supported by others.
- Negative youth groups displaying the impact of the neo-Nazi wave in the BRD or repeatedly engaging in riots, hooliganism, threats against positive youth, and resistance to state authorities, especially if they have connections to hostile individuals or such individuals join these groups.

For the operational service units, it is essential to recognize such phenomena early, classify them correctly, and quickly initiate effective political-operational measures in cooperation with state organs and social organizations to prevent a transition into political underground activity preventively.

Political-Ideological Subversion

A component of the enemy's subversion against real socialism, encompassing subversive attacks in the ideological field. The enemy aims to achieve subversive goals in a long-term, multi-stage process. These goals include undermining socialist consciousness or hindering its development, undermining the trust of broad population groups in the policies of communist parties and socialist states, inspiring anti-socialist behaviors up to the commission of state crimes, mobilizing hostile-negative forces in socialist states, developing a hostile ideological and personnel base in socialist states to inspire → political underground activity, and provoking dissatisfaction, unrest, passivity, and political uncertainty among broad population groups. The subversive attacks characterized by anti-communism and anti-Sovietism serve the implementation of the imperialist global strategy and are primarily directed against the political power of the working class and its Marxist-Leninist parties, Marxism-Leninism as the worldview of the working class in its entirety, the role and position of the USSR and the CPSU in the socialist community of states and in the peace struggle, proletarian internationalism, and the unity and cohesion of the European and international communist and workers' movement.

The political-ideological subversion ultimately aims to erode the ideological substance and constitutional foundations in socialist states to initiate the restoration of imperialist conditions in these states. Political-ideological subversion is carried out by special organs, facilities, and forces of imperialist states, the centers of political-ideological subversion. To achieve their goals, they use the latest knowledge and achievements of science (e.g., psychology, sociology, communication science) and technology, especially in the field of mass media. They employ a variety of means and methods, particularly mass manipulation, such as spreading lies and half-truths, falsifying and distorting facts, etc., and the intensified use of contacts within the framework of the → enemy's contact policy/contact activity. The subversive ideological attacks and the resulting effects vary greatly depending on individual and societal conditions processed in people's consciousness, ranging from changes in consciousness, readiness to act, to active actions in line with the enemy's objectives.

Political-ideological subversion contradicts the norms of international law. It is characterized by → interference in the internal affairs of socialist states. The realization of the goals of political-ideological subversion involves increasingly close cooperation between the centers of political-ideological subversion and imperialist intelligence services.

Politically-Operative Reconnaissance Work

Politically-operative work of various operational units of the MfS within and after the → operational area.

The main component of politically-operative reconnaissance work is the reconnaissance of the main administration reconnaissance of the MfS against hostile centers and main targets using specific conspiratorial means and methods outside the borders of the DDR. Objectives of the politically-operative reconnaissance work of the main administration reconnaissance of the MfS are:

- timely and reliably clarifying the plans, intentions, agencies, means, and methods of the enemy that endanger or impair the security and interests of the DDR, the socialist community of states, the communist world movement, and other revolutionary forces and preventing surprises in the political, military, scientific, and scientific-technical fields, contributing to the clarification and dismantling of → hostile bases and agencies in the DDR, the socialist community of states, the communist world movement, and other revolutionary forces,

- obtaining exact knowledge about the main enemy centers, the hostile potential, and the contradictions within the enemy camp, and carrying out offensive measures against hostile centers and hostile forces operating in the operational area,
- strengthening and consolidating the international position of socialism and its allies in the class struggle with imperialism, supporting the offensive peace policy of the socialist community of states, promoting anti-imperialist movements, forces, and organizations, and helping progressive governments in developing countries to consolidate their power,
- supporting the policy of the party and state leadership aimed at economic and military strengthening and further increasing the well-being of the people,
- ensuring the security of the foreign representations of the DDR and DDR citizens in non-socialist foreign countries. To achieve these objectives, state-conscious citizens of the DDR and suitable persons from imperialist states and developing countries are recruited as IM to fulfill politically-operative assignments. The reconnaissance work is carried out in coordination and cooperation with the other operational lines and operational units of the MfS, especially with those that also have tasks outside the borders of the DDR within the framework of their case-related and personal politically-operative work in and after the operational area.

Politically-Operative Work

The activity of the operational forces of the MfS based on the class mandate of the SED to realize the → security requirements of socialist society.

It is part of the → security policy of the SED, essentially conspiratorial political work to protect and strengthen the DDR, ensure its state security, and realize international relations and commitments in the class struggle, especially against the subversion of the enemy. Politically-Operative Work serves to fulfill the following → main tasks of the MfS:

- Clarification of the plans and intentions of the enemy,
- Preventive prevention and combating of subversive actions by hostile persons within the DDR (internal security),
- Organization of work in and after the operational area,
- Cooperation with state and economic leading organs and social organizations and institutions to increase order and security in all social areas and to eliminate favorable conditions and prevent harmful actions while constantly ensuring the primacy of prevention.

The specific goals and ways to realize Politically-Operative Work are defined in the official regulations of the MfS, whose consistent, self-responsible, and creative realization is directed at

- offensive penetration into the conspiracy of hostile forces and opposing agencies,
- preventive security and operational processing of unstable, wavering, and hostile-negative groups and individuals, especially from the target groups of the enemy,
- focused security of operationally significant areas, objects, territories, and processes,
- clarification of the question "Who is who?" for operationally significant persons,
- processing recognized enemy activities or suspicion of enemy activities in OV and OPK,
- incident investigation,

- ensuring the security of leading representatives of the DDR and their guests,
- ensuring the secrecy, conspiracy, and security of operational forces, means, and methods, as well as the objects and facilities of the MfS,
- supporting the activities of leading party and state officials through timely information. Politically-Operative Work is realized through
- the operational forces (operational employees, officers in special deployment, and IM/GMS),
- the politically-operative processes, means, and methods (IM work as the core of Politically-Operative Work, security checks, OPK, process handling, investigation, observation, investigation activities, passport control, and search activities, etc.),
- the operational-technical means and methods,
- the management of Politically-Operative Work.

Political-Operative Conspiracy

A fundamental principle of political-operative work that ensures superiority over subversive enemy actions and the security-political effectiveness of the MfS activities. The conspiracy is characterized by:

- The use of secret, hidden forces, means, and methods from the enemy and the public,
- The concealment of political-operative plans, intentions, and measures,
- Active and offensive actions to surprise, deceive, distract, and misinform the enemy.

Conspiracy is based on the revolutionary combat experiences of the international workers' movement in confrontation with the bourgeois power and repression apparatus. It is always integrated into the struggle for power or securing the political power of the working class and must never be judged or utilized independently of this political goal. The political-operative conspiracy serves particularly to:

- Gain and use operationally significant information and evidence,
- Actively implement security-political necessary societal changes,
- Ensure the security and operational capacity of unofficial collaborators (IM) and other operative forces and facilities,
- Prepare and conduct operative processes to uncover, push back, and eliminate the enemy,
- Apply the entire tactical and technical chekist arsenal.

For the behavior of all operative forces, rules of conspiracy generally apply, and their adherence is required by official regulations. Additionally, every political-operative task and its realization conditions modify and supplement the fundamental rules. When enforcing conspiracy as an essential aspect of political-operative leadership activity and chekist education, both the willingness to act conspiratorially based on attitude and the ability to do so must be assessed and developed. The principles of secrecy and vigilance are closely related to conspiracy but must not be reduced to them.

Political-Operative Vigilance

A norm of behavior and the resulting conduct in politically operative work, characterized by focusing attention on phenomena and events (or signs thereof) that can endanger state → security or are otherwise of security-political significance, and by general readiness and preparedness to respond effectively to security threats.

Political-operative vigilance is a particularly pronounced and content-specific type of political vigilance, which, according to Article 23 of the Constitution, demands all citizens honorably protect peace, the socialist homeland, and its achievements. Educating all citizens in vigilance is an important contribution to implementing the → security policy of the Party. By developing mass vigilance, important prerequisites for solving politically operative tasks are simultaneously created.

Political-operative vigilance is directed towards recognizing signs that signal enemy activities, enemy-favoring circumstances in connection with ensuring social order and discipline, the behavior of operationally interesting individuals, and the constant critical examination of one's own behavior. It includes active measures to further examine such signs and to maintain orderly and security-stabilizing conditions.

Vigilance is closely related to → conspiracy and → confidentiality in politically operative work.

Prejudice

Emotionally negatively or positively tinted → attitude that impairs the objectivity of recognition and the appropriateness of behavior. Prejudices can exist, for example, towards persons, groups of people, matters, theories, and institutions. They arise primarily from unjustified generalizations of personal experiences, uncritical adoption of others' opinions, and distorted application of scientific knowledge. Usually, the convenience in thinking and a specific attitude pattern are promoting conditions. Prejudices should be considered not only as individual but also as group-specific phenomena since relatively similar prejudices can develop among the members of a group and become group norms. For the members of the MfS, the problem of prejudices is significant in several ways: in clarifying operationally interesting individuals and groups (prejudices as components of their negative or hostile attitudes); in recruiting individuals for collaboration (prejudices as inhibiting factors for recruitment or later activity), but also in the education and self-education of employees to avoid missteps in work and disruptions in collective relationships caused by prejudicial effects. Moreover, it is the task of → public relations work to dismantle existing prejudices against the MfS and to contribute to forming correct convictions.

The use and creation of prejudices (attitude stereotypes) belong to the methodical arsenal of political-ideological diversion.

Prevention

As an essential element of the security policy of the party, a general task of all state organs, security and law enforcement organs, economic leading organs, enterprises, and institutions, as well as social organizations. It is an integrated part of the politically operative work of all service units of the MfS.

The preventive activity of the MfS is aimed at recognizing threats to state → security and the occurrence of damage-causing situations and actions in time, preventing them, eliminating causes and favorable conditions for state crimes, or paralyzing them in their effectiveness, supporting and strengthening the responsibility of the aforementioned organs for preventive activities. The main areas of prevention in the activities of the MfS are the preventive politically operative work of all service units of the MfS, the preventive cooperation of the politically operative service units with the partners in their area of responsibility, and the public relations work of the MfS.

The social and politically operative effectiveness of preventive work is measured, in particular, by whether and to what extent it has been possible:

- To recognize and prevent intended, prepared, or planned hostile-negative activities already in the initial phase,
- To prevent recognized hostile-negative actions, especially working in such a way that significant negative socially harmful effects do not occur,
- To recognize individuals who have come into conflict with the development of the DDR and offer favorable starting points to the enemy and to secure them in such a way that they are not misused and gradually regained for a positive social position,

- To recognize and overcome situations that can cause, in particular, accidents, explosions, fires, etc.,
- To disintegrate, isolate, and eliminate recognized hostile active individuals/groups, thus preventing them from causing further socially dangerous effects,
- Through qualified information activities, to support the policy of the party and state leadership, as well as the measures of the district and county leaderships of the SED and the subordinate party organizations in the political and political-ideological confrontation,
- Through operational cooperation, to achieve a demonstrably higher effect to ensure order and security.

The core of prevention is to recognize and prevent hostile-negative activities and threatening situations of politically operative significance in time. Successful prevention is achieved mainly when it is possible to prevent intended, prepared, or planned hostile-negative actions from unfolding or being realized. This requires two main prerequisites: First, it is necessary to have IM/GMS placed where plans, intentions, undertakings, or activities of a subversive nature are forged, or threatening situations can develop. The preventive deployment of IM/GMS according to the security requirements of the socialist society and the resulting priority areas is a fundamental requirement for achieving politically operative work results of the above evaluation criteria. Second, successful prevention requires the timely initiation of offensive, creative, and damage-preventive measures and control over their implementation to bring about socially and politically positive changes. Special importance is attached to the initiation of damage-preventive measures within the framework of operational person control and case processing; to being fully prepared for the occurrence of politically operative significant incidents; to regaining individuals already involved in subversive activities in one way or another; to targeted, systematic, and differentiated cooperation with other protection and security organs, particularly to influence ensuring high public order and security, and to developing more effective public relations work, focusing on differentiated influence on the enemy image transmission, increasing vigilance, and developing and deepening security-political thinking.

Preventive Conversation with Youths

A method applied in preventive work by own or forces of political-operative cooperation to prevent youths from endangering public order and security or engaging in other hostile-negative actions through direct influence.

Preventive conversations are required when youths are operationally involved or could reasonably be expected to be involved in securing significant social objects, territories, processes, events, persons, or groups, or when youth associations pose criminal risks and potential enemy misuse.

Preventive conversations aim to enforce socially appropriate behavior, prevent socially inappropriate behavior and its potential transformation into hostile activity, reduce or eliminate the causes and conditions for such behavior, specifically dissolve or transform negative youth groups, and obtain operationally significant information.

Preventive conversations must be planned, prepared in terms of content and organization, and conducted tactically in the most effective conversation conditions adapted to the personality development of the youth, so that demands for socially appropriate behavior are recognized and seriously accepted by the youth through persuasion, granting personal help, instruction, and announcement of controls.

Public Relations

As an important subarea of political-operative work corresponding to the main task of the MfS, public relations work is essentially an offensive, political-ideological enlightenment and educational work necessary for strengthening the socialist state and legal order in the fight against the imperialist enemy. This is carried out by certain units, leaders, and employees of the MfS tasked with it. Public relations work is conducted based on the decisions of the party and the orders, instructions, and guidelines of the comrade minister, strictly maintaining conspiracy and secrecy.

Its goals are:

- To expose the criminal and peace-threatening nature as well as the plans, intentions, means, and methods of the enemy and his class nature.
- To educate the working class and all working people in a scientifically grounded and emotionally effective manner to hate and fight against imperialism and its intelligence services.
- To convey a truthful and politically-ideologically correct image of the protective and security function of our organ, effective in the interest of peace and security and based on socialist legality.
- To strengthen, above all, the trust relationship of the citizens to the organs of the MfS, thereby developing the prerequisites for active cooperation between the MfS and the working people in solving the tasks of the MfS and thereby also strengthening the informal basis of political-operative work.
- To cultivate revolutionary and Chekist traditions and to spread the role of the MfS in the fight against the enemy in an educationally effective form in public.
- To generate high revolutionary vigilance, to increase the sense of responsibility and duty for maintaining and improving order and security in all areas, and to further develop and consolidate

political basic convictions such as pride in our socialist achievements and the willingness to defend and protect what has been achieved, especially the love for the Soviet Union.

Forms of public relations work include: forums, lectures, exhibitions, military-political cabinets and events, press conferences, presentations in the press, scientific journals, brochures, books, films, radio and television, cooperation and professional consultation of relevant departments of the MfS with journalists, scientists, artists dealing with issues of the MfS in their work, etc.

Quarters for Negatively Decadent Youth

Premises used by negatively decadent youth for various purposes and therefore politically-operatively significant. Such quarters are used, among other things:

- For meetings of like-minded individuals, fulfilling private leisure needs (drinking, feasting, orgies),
- For exchanging opinions, passing on messages for planned meetings or events to be attended, and other agreements,
- For temporary accommodation or overnight stays, sometimes avoiding police registration requirements,
- For temporary hiding places for individuals seeking to evade control and searches,
- For maintaining connections within negatively decadent groups like hitchhikers, negative groups, etc.

Such quarters can include:

- Apartments of negatively decadent youth,
- Vacant apartments in buildings slated for demolition,
- Single-family homes with adjacent outbuildings,
- Unused barns or dilapidated farmsteads,
- Garden sheds, etc.,
- Overnight accommodations for hitchhikers in church facilities.

Due to their danger and operational significance, such quarters used by negatively decadent youth must be promptly liquidated. This can be done through:

- Immediate influence on vacating the apartment or liquidating the quarters,
- Involvement of the housing administration, hygiene and other state organs.

Individuals providing such quarters to negatively decadent youth are to be operatively processed.

Ranger

Imperialist term for lone fighters belonging to special units of NATO troops who carry out military or subversive actions, usually in small groups, during open military conflicts and covert wars. As lone fighters for the execution of subversive actions, Rangers receive, in addition to basic military training as infantrymen, specialized training in close combat, reconnaissance, radio operation, and parachuting. They are trained in military topography and medical care and are especially drilled to "kill," commit murders, carry out bombings and assaults, and not shy away from any crime, however heinous, to survive.

The subversive activities of Rangers typically follow four main aspects: reconnaissance, diversion and terror, psychological influence on the population, and organizing or supporting subversive groups.

It is assumed that imperialist intelligence services have forces with ranger-like training.

Recovery

A method of preventive political-operative work by the MfS.

The content of recovery is to use appropriate political-operative measures, as well as ideological, moral, and other influences, to shake and reduce the anti-socialist positions of individuals who have slipped into enemy-negative ideological positions or have already acted enemy-negatively due to enemy influences. The goal of recovery is to lead these individuals to abandon their enemy-negative position and adopt at least a loyal attitude and behavior toward the socialist state and social order.

Recovery requires:

- Careful selection and determination of the most suitable person for recovery. The person must have points of approach that allow the initiation of recovery measures that achieve a high political and social benefit,
- Comprehensive and thorough clarification of the candidate's personality, especially the causes and conditions for slipping into the enemy-negative position and possible points of approach for initiating recovery measures,
- Use of trusted individuals,
- Initiation of measures to eliminate or mitigate enemy-negative influencing factors,
- Initiation of confidence-building measures.

Recovery as a process is considered successful if there are objective indications that the person has recognized their misuse by the enemy and is willing to draw appropriate conclusions from their previous behavior.

Recruitment Proposal

A binding document for preparing and conducting recruitment as a result of systematic processing of the IM preliminary stage. It includes:

- The personal details of the IM candidate,
- The justification for the need for recruitment and the intended direction and category of deployment,
- The assessment of the IM candidate, particularly their suitability, expected reliability, and willingness for conspiratorial

collaboration, including contradictory and possibly counteracting factors,
- The manner of becoming aware of the IM candidate and other significant aspects for ensuring conspiracy and confidentiality,
- The factors to be particularly considered in the future informal collaboration arising from the IM candidate's age and personal maturity, social status, affiliation to a specific national or religious community, and other characteristics,
- The recruitment plan, particularly addressing the scheduled summoning, the intended recruitment basis and the tactic of the recruitment conversation based on it, the organization of the commitment, the possible participation of a superior, the local and temporal conditions, and the future assurance of the conspiratorial connection with the IM and further problems to be considered in the initial phase of collaboration.

Registration

Centralized record-keeping of operative processes, investigation processes, IM preliminaries, IM cases, OPK files, GMS files, security processes, and about the operative responsible employee of an operative service unit. The basis of registration is the decision to create the process, preliminary, or file. Registration is carried out by assigning a binding registration number by the recording service unit of the MfS.

Relationship of Trust

The quality of interpersonal relationships that, due to complex, individually different psychological phenomena, leads to a one-sided or mutual preference and special recognition in certain areas of life. A relationship of trust develops mainly from knowledge about the partner, emotional attachment to them, and an attitude of reliance on them.

In politically operative activities, a relationship of trust is typically referred to between the operational employee and the IM, where it is aimed for the IM to have complete trust in the operational employee, while the operational employee must not overlook the aspect of security and control in their relationship with the IM. Between the IM and the operationally interesting person, a confidential relationship is usually referred to, expressing that the operationally interesting person has complete trust in the IM, while the IM pretends to trust them.

Relocation of IM

A political-operational method for the permanent or temporary deployment of reliable and specially trained IM from the DDR in the operational area.

Relocated IM are used to carry out particularly demanding political-operational tasks, whose fulfillment significantly influences the effectiveness and security of working with IM in the operational area.

The form of relocation depends on the operational objective, the objective possibilities, and the subjective conditions of the relocation candidate.

The relocation is particularly characterized by the fact that the relocated IM must be legalized in the operational area to enable them to solve their operational tasks covertly.

The relocation is to be carried out based on special guidelines and instructions.

Reporting System

A system regulated by the reporting order within the MfS, ensuring the prompt, current, truthful, and comprehensive informing of leaders about reportable political-operational matters. This system is a fundamental basis for effectively conducting leadership activities. The reporting order establishes the requirements for → operational reports, the reporting obligation, the senders and recipients of operational reports, and the methods of their transmission. It also specifies the responsibilities of leaders and the MfS members they designate for implementing an effective operational reporting system.

Information on operationally significant matters is urgently needed for:

- The continuous and current assessment of the political-operational situation,
- Timely and well-founded decision-making for directing political-operational work,
- Decisions on initiating political-operational measures to clarify and address the operational matters underlying the reports, as well as to prevent or mitigate dangers, damages, and other negative consequences,

The effective organization of → political-operational cooperation and → coordination,

- Systematic and timely informing of senior party and state officials, and thus must be promptly transmitted to superiors and other designated recipients.

Re-Recruitment

A special form of → recruitment of IM, applied to persons who carry out hostile activities on direct orders from intelligence services and other subversive centers, institutions, organizations, and forces against the DDR and the revolutionary main forces.

Re-recruitment requires thorough clarification of the recruitment candidate and particularly the creation of circumstances that firmly bind the recruitment candidates to the partner in education and highly likely compromise them with their principals.

The following principles must be particularly observed in re-recruitment:

- Disclosure and development of verifiable secret information by the recruitment candidate that binds them and shows their honesty,
- Implementation of special measures to ensure conspiracy that prevent the detection of re-recruitment by the mentioned institutions,
- Intensive, systematic control and verification of the recruitment candidate or IM,
- Proof that collaboration with the MfS is advantageous for the recruitment candidate, but refusal has negative consequences for them.

Responsiveness

Collective term for the individual susceptibility, willingness to receive, and openness of a person to oral, written, or generally understandable stimuli and information such as suggestions, demands, orders, etc. Responsiveness is also commonly understood as the willingness to respond to such stimuli with certain behaviors or individual actions. Responsiveness depends primarily on the significance of the stimulus or demand for the personality, the manner of transmission (emotional, rational), the current condition of the personality and its inner model, as well as general life experience and the current situation. Additionally, responsiveness is influenced by general excitability (emotional responsiveness) conditioned by temperament qualities and emotional equipment, as well as mental excitability (rational responsiveness) dependent on insight and cognitive ability. In operational work, the different responsiveness must be considered when recruiting IM and GMS, issuing orders, establishing and using official contacts, conducting investigations, and deploying cover stories.

Return Connection

Connection between former DDR citizens who left the DDR by illegal border crossing or with state permission and took permanent residence in non-socialist states or West Berlin, and individuals who have their permanent residence in the DDR. Return connections are used by the enemy, particularly for influencing in the context of inspiring or organizing illegal border crossings or unlawful requests for resettlement, recruiting smuggling candidates, creating enemy bases in the DDR, or for intelligence activities by imperialist intelligence services.

Return connections arise from existing ties in family or acquaintance circles and in leisure and work areas, including former joint studies or other former activities. Such former connections are referred to as return connections when the former DDR citizen himself or through enemy organs or forces from the operational area makes or is highly likely to make contact. Such connections can also be activated by the DDR citizen. In political-operative work, especially the operatively significant return connections must be worked out and placed under differentiated control.

Revanchist Organizations

Social organizations in the imperialist power structure whose declared goal is to regain territories and spheres of influence lost in wars of aggression and to seek revenge for the defeat suffered. They disregard the changes resulting from World War II and aim to reverse them. Their claims are contrary to international law. During the Cold War, a widespread and deeply layered network of organized revanchism emerged in the BRD, in the form of homeland associations, expellee organizations, their youth organizations, special institutions, and establishments, whose policies against détente are particularly directed against the countries of the socialist community of states. These forces' actions are characterized by extreme, militant anti-communism, anti-

Soviet agitation, and propaganda against the Warsaw Pact states. Contrary to the letter and spirit of treaties between the BRD and socialist states on the inviolability of existing borders in Europe, these forces insist on their "revision" and "change of the status quo." Revanchist organizations are part of the organizational base of the most aggressive circles of BRD imperialism and are in close contact with all system-supporting parties and state organs. They maintain particularly intensive connections with right-wing parties and groups, militarism, and neo-Nazism.

Organized revanchism is still tolerated, supported, and co-financed by state funds in the BRD. The various revanchist organizations in the BRD are united under umbrella organizations such as the "Bund der Vertriebenen - Vereinigte Landsmannschaften und Landesverbände e.V."

Revanchist organizations provide their connections, knowledge, and apparatus for subversive activities against socialist states.

Revelation of Suspects to Unofficial Collaborators (IMs)

Fragmentary, partial, or complete deliberate disclosure of facts about planned, prepared, or committed criminal acts by the suspect to an IM. A revelation occurs when the suspect credibly informs the IM that they intend to commit or have already committed a crime, or when they disclose to the IM the goals, intentions, or plans they pursued/pursue with a crime, the motives and attitudes underlying their criminal actions, how and with whose help they committed/plan to commit the crime, or when the suspect discloses the names of accomplices to the IM or informs them about connections to hostile agencies and forces in non-socialist foreign countries that they themselves have or know from other persons.

The revelation is usually based on confidential relationships between the suspect and the IM. It generally occurs when the suspect intends to involve the IM in anti-state activities or induce them to carry out subversive actions or when the suspect expects some other benefit from it.

The information provided by the suspect through a revelation must be thoroughly checked and substantiated or refuted with information and evidence. The revelation places high demands on the realization of the → extraction of IMs from the processing of operative processes.

Riot

An assembly of persons that disrupts public order and safety. A riot crime under § 217 StGB occurs when individuals participate in such an assembly and do not immediately leave it upon the security authorities' or other competent state organs' request. Riots can develop into dangerous attacks against state security, especially if the individuals act with hostile motivation. In connection with political highlights, major events, etc., the enemy intends to organize or inspire riots to test the nature of state intervention, provoke security authorities, and use their intervention as a pretext for hostile attacks within the framework of political-ideological diversion.

Riot perpetrators are often adolescents and young adults.

Rules of Political-Operative Conspiracy

Behavioral norms developed in illegal revolutionary activity and chekist struggle against the enemy for practically considering and implementing the principles of → conspiracy, secrecy, and vigilance. The rules of conspiracy include:

- Constant awareness of acting as a member of the MfS and the enemy's interest in one's person,
- Careful control of one's behavior and critical assessment of each action and measure concerning enemy access possibilities,
- Attentive, variable, and as creative as possible preparation and execution of each action and avoidance of schematic and blinding routine,

- Realistic and lifelike concealment of operative actions and diversion of enemy interests,
- Prevention of revealing operative knowledge in all areas of life, consistent protection of political-operative secrets, and careful examination of the use and handling of operative information,
- Thorough and comprehensive assessment and evaluation of people involved in political-operative tasks or measures,
- Organization of work division and design of responsibilities and information flows that allow everyone to know only what they need to perform their tasks.

The rules of conspiracy are to be specified and extended in connection with preparing and executing political-operative tasks and their conditions.

Rumor

A verbal representation of a fact burdened with uncertainty for a specific group of people in the form of assertions, speculations, or distortions, whose truth or falsehood cannot generally be proven by the recipient. Rumors usually relate to societal events, individuals, or groups of people in the public eye. They are directly related to the respective concrete conditions and tie into prevailing needs, hopes, expectations, fears, and partly realistic statements, seemingly reducing the uncertainty about the fact. Rumors are quickly spread as special "news" or "sensations" through a chain of individuals. Characteristic changes in the content regarding simplification, structuring, and detailing often occur.

Rumor spreaders usually refer to authorities to achieve rapid and unexamined dissemination.

Spreading rumors is a method of political-ideological diversion. They are generated or picked up and disseminated by the centers of political-ideological diversion and intelligence services through contact policies/activities, press, radio, and television or by intermediaries. They aim at behavior-oriented impact on the recipient, pursuing specific objectives integrated into the political-ideological diversion, such as:

- Undermining the trust relationship between the population and the party and state leadership by defaming leading personalities,
- Influencing and undermining socialist consciousness by creating unrest, dissatisfaction, forms of passive resistance, and phenomena of disorganization and demoralization,
- Triggering hostile actions, especially in tension situations, through intensified manipulation,
- Protecting hostile agencies.

Due to these objectives, rumors are of varying degrees of operational interest.

Sabotage

State crime under § 104 of the Criminal Code (StGB). Sabotage is part of the system of enemy activities against the DDR and other socialist states. It is predominantly integrated into economic disruptive activities and is primarily organized and carried out by hostile individuals and groups from corporations and other capitalist enterprises, typically in close collaboration with them.

Sabotage can also be committed without connection to enemy agencies and forces of the imperialist system. Sabotage attacks the political and economic foundations of the socialist state and social order, as well as its national defence. Acts of sabotage are directed against the planned development of the national economy or individual branches or enterprises, the fulfillment of economic plans, the activities of state organs or social organizations, the defense capabilities or defense measures of the DDR, or the foreign economic measures of the socialist state by disrupting or disorganizing them.

Sabotage is mainly targeted at the primary tasks in the further development of the developed socialist society and the socialist economic integration, criminally exploiting the DDR's foreign economic relations with the non-socialist economic area.

Sabotage crimes are committed by abusing functions or professional positions or circumventing the resulting duties, often through misleading the responsible state or economic organs. Due to the complex nature of enemy activities, there are close connections between sabotage crimes integrated into economic disruptive activities and espionage crimes against the economy. Espionage crimes against the economy are often the starting point or part of sabotage crimes.

Sanction

1. Commonly used for confirmation, approval, recognition, consent (sanctioning a measure);
2. In a narrower sense, a system of measures of reward or punishment (praise and criticism) to regulate behaviors. Sanctions have educational functions (societal recognition or rejection), coordinating functions (guidance, steering of various actions by different people in one direction), informative functions (orientation to given political, professional, and moral standards). For the education of employees as well as IMs and GMSs, a whole system of differentiated measures and means for material and moral recognition of performances and for making insufficient performances or wrong behaviors materially and morally noticeable is available.

Secrecy Holder

Persons who store secrets in their consciousness as non-materialized information or items that store secrets by their nature and constitution (documents, writings, films, sound carriers, drawings, pictures, maps, symbols, signals, signs, etc.) or have them materialized within themselves (machines, weapons, facilities, devices, models, etc.). For secrecy protection, the political and moral attitude and maturity of personal secrecy holders, especially the responsible leaders for their protection, are crucial. They must not only keep the secrets they know confidential but also secure material (materialized) secrecy holders against unauthorized disclosure by complying with and enforcing applicable legal regulations.

Secrecy holders are targets of attacks by foreign powers, their institutions or representatives, intelligence services, or foreign organizations or their helpers and are thus an essential part of the political-operative counterintelligence work of the MfS. A distinction is made between holders of → state secrets and → service secrets.

Secret Intelligence Liaison System

The entirety of forces, means, and methods used by intelligence services to maintain the most stable and secure connection possible for transmitting information and items to the agent and vice versa.

The liaison system is a prerequisite and component of subversive cooperation between the headquarters and the agency.

Components of the liaison system, also referred to as types of liaison, include:

- Meetings of agency-leading intelligence officers or residents with their agents;
- Approaching agents by couriers or instructors;

Use of → Dead Letter Boxes (DLBs);

- Telephone connection (usually via automatic answering machines);
- Postal connection (usually through cover addresses);
- Radio connection.

All listed connections can be used either in isolation from each other or in combination.

Security

As a social phenomenon, it is a qualitative characteristic of social relationships and the human and material relationships and institutions existing or developing within them. It is expressed in how stable such relationships and institutions are against disturbances, how functional they prove under various conditions, and how effectively they can be protected from dangers. Security depends on the character of the respective social order and the extent of the socio-economic, political, and ideological conditions within it. It concerns the interests and goals of the classes, particularly regarding the preservation and expansion of economic and political power relations or their transformation, the security of the existence of the respective classes and their political organization, and the shaping of interstate relations. Therefore, security has a class character. In socialism, security is the expression of overcoming class antagonism internally; it manifests in the growing stability and dynamics of society and the security of all its members. At the same time, it is the expression of international class struggle; it is evident in the results of the struggle to push back the imperialist policy directed against peace and socialism, in the implementation of peaceful coexistence. Security is anchored in the goals of the socialist society and takes on the character of a fundamental value of socialism. The security of the socialist society is primarily ensured through the further development and strengthening of the socialist society itself. Significant tasks include the preventive prevention, detection, and combating of enemy attacks on society or parts of it, as well as eliminating other dangers and disturbances that impair social development. The security of the socialist society is created, maintained, or increased as a state through the actions of all people, especially through the division of labor organized activities of state protection and security organs in a comprehensive social process.

Security Forces

Members of the MfS acting to secure people, objects, areas, items, and events. Security forces are trained according to the politically operative task to recognize changes in the situation during the preparation and execution of actions and deployments, to ensure public order and security, to detect and prevent hostile-negative actions, and to identify and isolate hostile-negative individuals in or near the area of action.

Security forces are distinguished into:

- Military-operational forces, who are uniformed and carry out visible security and control measures for the public,
- Politically-operative forces, who realize recognizable tasks in civilian clothes,
- Specialists, who carry out special tasks to secure or at event locations and usually act undercover.

The members of the MfS can be supported by unofficial employees of our organ and selected forces from other security and protection organs, state organs, and social organizations while maintaining conspiracy and secrecy.

Self-Reporter

An individual recruited by an imperialist intelligence service or other enemy agencies or forces who, for various motives, turns themselves in to socialist security agencies and provides information about their subversive activities. Motives for self-reporting can include: enemy assignment, honest intention, personal reasons like egoism, material interests, etc. Reporting to security agencies can occur directly or through other state organs, institutions, societal forces, or individuals. Self-reporters sometimes offer themselves for cooperation with the MfS (→ Self-Offerer). The targeted offering of spies under the guise of self-reporters is a method used by imperialist intelligence services to establish contact with socialist security agencies, learn about their working methods, and infiltrate the IM system (→ Double Agent). The decision to refrain from criminal liability for self-reporters is generally regulated in § 25 StGB.

Single Leadership

Basic leadership principle in the MfS. According to the principle of single leadership, the leader bears undivided responsibility in their area of responsibility to ensure that all politically-operative tasks are fulfilled, subordinate leaders and employees are educated and enabled to fulfill these tasks, and develop into Chekist personalities. This responsibility of the leader includes their → authority to issue directives and control.

Single leadership is the specific form of implementing democratic centralism in the MfS and embodies the unity of political, politically-operative, politically-ideological, economic, and administrative leadership. It demands and promotes military discipline and strict order and provides space for the conscious and creative participation of all MfS members in fulfilling the assigned tasks.

In implementing single leadership, leaders have the right and duty to issue directives to subordinate leaders and employees and to issue orders or other → official regulations. They must conduct necessary consultations with knowledgeable MfS members in preparing official regulations and directives and develop the initiative, readiness, and capability of the collective in their implementation.

Skill, operative

Personality trait of operative forces, which as an automated component of conscious actions significantly contributes to the perfect mastery of operational activities. Skills are developed through practice and training of operational activities, whereby physical and mental components of action are automated to run securely despite reduced control by consciousness. They then ensure a smooth flow of operational actions, reduce effort and tension, relieve attention, and enable better orientation towards the course and goal of operational actions. The acquisition of skills requires systematic knowledge acquisition, positive motivational conviction, and a self-critical attitude towards practice results.

Social Employee for Security (GMS)

Citizens of the DDR with a publicly known state-conscious attitude and stance who agree to cooperate confidentially with the MfS and participate in solving various political-operative tasks according to their capabilities and qualifications. Social employees for security provide valuable support to the operative basis, a reservoir for recruiting IM, and developing cadres for the MfS.

Working with social employees for security aims at further enhancing internal security in their area of responsibility, particularly by effectively supplementing information gathering for continuously assessing and managing the political-operative situation and comprehensively implementing the MfS's preventive and damage-preventing work.

Social Harmfulness

A material property of offenses marked as offenses in § 1 Abs. 2 StGB, below the threshold of → societal danger, characterizing their objective harm to society or individual citizens. Social harmfulness reflects the relationship of the offense to the rights and interests of the socialist society or its citizens and the nature and depth of the contradiction to the social fundamental requirements of the socialist society. It indicates the severity of the attack on the socialist society or its citizens, expressing the specific antisocial nature of the offense.

The precise examination and determination of the degree of social harmfulness of politically-operative significant general criminal offenses in political-operative and investigative work is a key prerequisite for realizing individual criminal responsibility. Determining social harmfulness should be based on the specific nature of the individual elements of the → act of the offense, including the → perpetrator's personality. Social harmfulness only includes circumstances that are crime-related and have a real impact on the antisocial nature of the offense.

Socialist Economic Integration; Political-Operative Security

A complex of political-operative measures for the reliable protection of development-determining projects and processes of socialist economic integration. Security is provided to ensure comprehensive safety during the development-determining projects and processes of socialist economic integration and to prevent any subversive attacks by imperialist centers and forces through the extensive exclusion of hostile and other socially harmful influences or effects on their planned, effective implementation, and to prevent the subversive misuse of persons deployed for realizing the tasks of socialist economic integration. The political-operative counterintelligence work determined by this goal focuses on ensuring that the DDR can fulfill its obligations within the framework of socialist economic integration without disruptions. The security of development-determining projects and processes of socialist economic integration is integrated into the overall political-operative security of the economy and follows the priority principle. The state's security interests in development-determining projects and processes of socialist economic integration and the long-term, prospective-oriented actions of hostile centers and forces against them require organizing political-operative security work according to long-term, perspective-oriented → security and processing concepts. Based on the state's security interests in socialist economic integration, political-operative counterintelligence work should focus on the following priority complexes:

- enforcing the decisions of the Party and the Council of Ministers of the DDR to realize the specific tasks of the DDR contained in the target programs of the RGW and the derived (general) agreements and in the specialization and cooperation program of production between the DDR and the USSR until 1990,
- bilateral and multilateral government agreements and treaties for research and production cooperation or specialization, on investment participation in establishing significant production capacities, developing trade and cooperation in planning, finance, and credit relations,
- areas for the material provision of the socialist state community's defense readiness and selected tasks to be realized according to their significance in the respective political, economic, and military situation,
- bodies and institutions in the DDR significantly involved in preparing and implementing the economic policy strategy coordinated within the RGW.

The political-operative work to secure development-determining integration projects and processes should primarily be organized in the following main directions within the framework of qualified political-operative groundwork:

1. Protecting politically-operative significant persons deployed for fulfilling the tasks of socialist economic integration.
2. Ensuring reliable secrecy protection.
3. Preventive prevention, uncovering, and combating disruptions and damages in realizing development-determining integration projects and processes.
4. Political-operative security of significant consultations and conferences of RGW bodies, ZZ work, and other organizational forms of socialist economic integration on the DDR territory.

Effective security work requires synchronizing political-operative counterintelligence work in all main directions and enforcing the security-political responsibility of state and economic leaders, offensively using all potentials of socialist law. Further deepening cooperation with the security organs of friendly socialist states to secure development-determining integration projects and processes is indispensable.

Socialist Security Policy

A component of the party's policy. It is aimed at consciously implementing the objective security requirements of the socialist society. Security policy is determined by the objective and universally valid law of protecting the achievements of socialism against the attacks of external and internal enemies in an inseparable connection with all other objective laws of the socialist revolution and its current requirements, the goals of the working class, its Marxist-Leninist party, and the socialist state. At the center of security policy is the protection and further consolidation of the working-class power and its effective use for the preventive prevention and elimination of all disturbances in socialist development. Due to the objective inseparable interweaving of economy, politics, and ideology with security issues, security policy is aimed at the holistic development of socialism. Security policy is characterized by the following features:

- Security policy has a peace-creating, peace-preserving, and peace-commanding character. By uncovering the causes and goals of imperialist confrontation policy and the associated aggressive plans and intentions, it contributes significantly to ensuring the preservation and securing of peace, supporting and enforcing the peace policy of the Warsaw Pact states, maintaining the defense potential at the necessary level, and excluding any surprises from outside and inside.
- Security policy has a revolutionary-protective character. With its effects of preserving, maintaining, and consolidating socialist achievements, it simultaneously achieves activating and mobilizing effects on the overall social development process of socialism.

- Security policy has a humanistic character. This is primarily visible through the social content and social objective of this policy. The protection of the socialist society and its overall undisturbed development, as well as the individual citizen, from very concrete, acute, or potential threats, dangers, and damages, characterizes security policy as profoundly humanistic.
- Security policy has a societal character. Ensuring social stability and security in all areas as an inherent part of the social movement itself must be realized under the leadership of the working-class party through the active actions of all people. The party addresses its security policy to the protection and security organs, all other state organs, institutions, combines, enterprises, social organizations, all citizens, and their communities. The effectiveness of security policy is inseparable from the further development and perfection of socialist democracy.
- Security policy has an internationalist character. The dialectic of national and international requires that security policy serves both the security of the respective socialist state and its citizens and must be conceived, planned, led, and realized from an internationalist perspective. This results from the universality and internationalist character of the laws of transition from capitalism to communism, as well as from the threats of "international capital," especially its internationally organized and led counter-revolutionary activities against socialism.
- Security policy is an expression of socialist legality. The consistent implementation of socialist law is an essential element in realizing security policy. In the legal provisions of the socialist state, fundamental requirements for implementing security policy are reflected. Laws and other legal regulations norm the social relations to be protected in accordance with the level of social development and the party's decisions and orientations. Thus, the social relations to be protected are given the necessary stability and their revolutionary dynamic further development is ensured. The socialist state uses the law in its entirety for the consistent

implementation of security policy. All branches of socialist law, as well as international agreements, contain corresponding security policy tasks in socialist society.

- Security policy is partisan, objective, and scientific. It is in full agreement with the objective fundamental interests of the working class and serves their implementation. It is determined by the objective connections, laws, and conditions of historical development, the concrete-historical class struggle situation, the objective conditions, and the resulting objective security requirements. As a component of the party's policy, security policy is founded on the ideological basis of Marxism-Leninism. Its overall conception, orientations towards practical results, and individual security policy tasks include the scientific principles of Marxism-Leninism.

From the differentiated content of security policy arise the following relatively independent components:

- Ensuring national defense, including securing the state border,
- Ensuring state security,
- Ensuring and consolidating order, discipline, and security in all social areas. There are the closest connections between them.

Based on the unified class mandate of the party to the protection and security organs, the MfS must primarily prevent, uncover, and effectively combat all subversive attacks of the enemy, especially on the defense capability of socialism, the undisturbed implementation of the party's economic strategy, and the ideological foundations of the working-class worldview, and thus make the greatest possible contribution to ensuring the state sovereignty and territorial integrity of the DDR and the overall realization of security policy.

Source

An information carrier used in the political-operative work of the MfS to obtain operatively significant information.

A distinction is made between unofficial sources and official sources. Unofficial sources are primarily the IM and GMS, but also operative means used specifically to obtain operatively significant information.

Official sources are individuals used in the context of cooperation or other official forms to obtain operatively significant information, and official records, materials, documents, publications, archives, information storage (e.g., the DVP), the daily press, magazines, etc.

State Demonstrative Measures

Offensive preventive activities by state organs that openly demonstrate the intent and strength of socialist state power with the goal of preventing hostile and other criminal actions, immediately effectively stopping them when they occur, and thus directly influencing order and security. State demonstrative measures are targeted actions by the People's Police (e.g., increased deployment of police forces), the MfS (e.g., demonstrative measures to unsettle or disrupt), the judicial authorities (e.g., accelerated proceedings for rowdy actions), and other state organs (e.g., issuing directives). The effectiveness of state demonstrative measures can be increased through targeted publications and other forms of → public relations work. State demonstrative measures are of particular importance in certain situations or on specific occasions where, based on experience or specific indications, hostile or other criminal actions (e.g., rowdiness, gatherings, provocations) are expected.

Subversion

A key component of imperialist strategy and policy. Subversion encompasses all those activities, actions, and operations inspired, organized, and conducted by specific organizations, institutions, and forces of imperialism with the aim of promoting and triggering counter-revolutionary processes, events, and developments, and supporting material and ideological war preparations, thus contributing to a shift in the balance of power in favor of imperialism.

The core of subversive activities is the undermining, destabilization, destruction, and ultimate elimination of the existing social conditions in socialist countries. Additionally, subversion targets the revolutionary workers' movement and other anti-imperialist forces in capitalist states, against nationally liberated states, and other progressive movements and political trends in these countries.

Subversion is incompatible with international law. Key forms of subversive activity include → espionage against all areas of societal life, → political-ideological diversion, adversary → contact policy/contact activities, organizing political → underground activities, inciting the population or parts of the population of socialist or nationally liberated states against their constitutional order, attempts to create an "internal → opposition," staging conspiracies, economic → disruptive activities, state-hostile → human trafficking, violent attacks against state borders, organizing coups and uprisings, launching large-scale smear and defamation campaigns, abusing mass media, and threatening and realizing → terror and other acts of violence.

To achieve the goals associated with subversion, imperialism utilizes a comprehensive and differentiated force potential, including:

- Imperialist intelligence services with their extensive networks of offices, residences, agencies, and auxiliary organs,
- Centers of political-ideological diversion, including the strategic orientation centers responsible for anti-communism, Eastern Europe, and DDR research, as well as imperialist mass media,

Criminal → human trafficking gangs,

- Special organizations, institutions, and forces primarily engaged in subversive and destabilizing activities against the socialist

society, partly from the Cold War era and partly formed specifically to exploit détente policy results,
- Institutions and forces organizing economic disruptive activities and other attacks against the socialist economy and integration,
- Revanchist organizations and so-called homeland associations,
- Right- and left-wing extremist and specifically terrorist organizations, groups, and forces,
- State and semi-state institutions with profiles exploitable for subversion,
- Legal positions of imperialism in socialist states,
- Hostile, negative, and politically ideologically wavering individuals and groups in socialist society.

Subversion employs various sophisticated, deceitful, brutal, and violent means and methods. Imperialism invests significant efforts to continuously perfect, diversify, and complete the subversive instrumentarium. This includes trends towards refinement and sophistication, as well as brutality and violence, coupled with efforts to perfectly disguise and obscure goals, backers, means, and methods.

Expressions of increasing brutality and violence in subversive actions include organizing border and other provocations, terrorist attacks against individuals and socially significant institutions, threats of murder against progressive politicians and citizens, anonymous and pseudonymous threats of violence, and the spectacular use of violent means and technical equipment.

The instrumentarium of subversion particularly includes intelligence methods, manipulation, disinformation, lies, and demagogy, psychological and ideological terrorization, promoting, supporting, and encouraging anti-socialist and counter-revolutionary forces, indirectly guiding ("careful external control") opposition groups, involving renegades, traitors, and former citizens of socialist states in subversive activities.

A crucial part of the subversion instrumentarium is the intelligence-controlled deployment of informers and agents. Their tasks include infiltrating and destabilizing progressive political organizations and groups, implementing measures in the organization of creeping counter-revolution, and participating in political, economic, and military espionage against socialist countries.

Subversive means and methods are complemented by actions corresponding to general criminal acts such as extortion, active and passive bribery, serious burglary, document forgery, drug and poison use, insurance fraud, foreign exchange manipulation, etc. The subversive instrumentarium is further characterized by the increasing abuse of contractually granted legal political, commercial, cultural, and other relations and opportunities, such as legal work contacts and information rights of privileged persons, and the misuse of company and bank representations and all forms of travel.

New developments in science and technology are increasingly being used for subversion, leading to the use of computer-controlled airborne and ground-based electronic reconnaissance and information systems for espionage, computers for storing detailed personal data, electronic devices for unnoticed analysis of behavioral characteristics of interest (advancements of the lie detector), etc.

System, hostile search

The entirety of organs, institutions, forces, means, and methods, as well as the related regulations for determining the whereabouts or travel routes and monitoring persons, finding objects or spaces in connection with the pursuit of criminal acts, suppression of democratic forces, organizing the subversive struggle of imperialist intelligence services against socialist states, and countering activities of socialist intelligence and security organs in the → operational area. The search is aimed at creating conditions for further measures by hostile intelligence and counterintelligence organs (e.g., observation, recruitment, arrest). In the BRD, particularly the following organs are involved in the hostile search system:

- Intelligence services, especially the Federal Office and the State Offices for the Protection of the Constitution,
- The Federal Criminal Police Office,
- The State Criminal Police Offices and other police organs of the federal states,
- The Federal Border Guard, especially the Border Protection Service,
- Customs investigation service and border customs service,
- Railway police, especially the search service of the German Federal Railway,
- The postal surveillance service,
- The Federal Motor Transport Authority,
- The foreigner authorities, etc.

The search system of the BRD is systematically expanded with significant financial resources. This includes introducing modern electronic data collection and transmission systems (INPOL, NADIS, ZEVIS, JURIS, etc.).

The counterintelligence organs of NATO states increasingly cooperate in search operations as needed.

Tension Indicators

A term used by the Federal Intelligence Service (Bundesnachrichtendienst) for characteristics that indicate fundamental changes in the military and political situation in the respective operational country. These include, among others, extraordinary actions by governments, reactions to significant domestic and foreign political events, and extraordinary actions by the population in the respective operational countries.

In principle, all spies of imperialist intelligence services receive the general order to report immediately and in the quickest way possible about recognized tension indicators. In its espionage instructions, the Federal Intelligence Service describes which tension indicators might be typical for the operational country, how to recognize them, and how to formulate and transmit the corresponding information.

Territorial Principle

A principle for the organizational structure of the MfS, whereby an operational service unit is responsible for protecting social development and ensuring state security in a specific territory (district, county, independent city, city district) in accordance with the state's territorial division. The territorial principle is implemented in the organizational structure of the MfS in unity with the principle of single leadership, the → focus principle, and the → line principle.

Terror

An essential expression of imperialism and the aggressive policy of imperialist states. As part of the system of hostile activities, terrorist crimes are primarily carried out by imperialist intelligence services and other hostile organizations, institutions, and forces against socialist states, national liberation movements, the working class in imperialist states, and other progressive forces. Out of misunderstanding the complexity of class struggle, certain left-extremist forces or splinter groups of national liberation movements also resort to terrorist means and methods. In the DDR, terrorist crimes are typically committed by hostile negative individuals under the direct or indirect influence of the enemy, particularly under the impact of political-ideological subversion. Terror in its various forms is characterized by brutal use of force or immediate threat of violence, such as the use of weapons, explosives, poisons, and other dangerous means and methods. Terrorist crimes can be directed against individuals, but also against objects and facilities. The objective of terror is to influence the psyche of people, e.g., to

- change or impair their attitudes and behavior in a hostile manner,
- deter socially active citizens from their activities,
- cause fear and panic among the population,
- exert extortionate pressure on state organ decisions, ultimately harming the socialist state and social order.

In the criminal sense, terror according to §§ 101, 102 StGB includes committing acts of violence (armed attacks, hostage-taking, explosions, arson, destruction, causing accidents) to resist the socialist state and social order or provoke unrest, as well as attacks on the lives or health of state or socially active citizens or other forms of violence against them to harm the DDR.

Terrorism

An extremely acute form of reactionary violence in class struggle, elevated to a political strategy.

Terrorism differs from other forms of political violence by pursuing the aim of intimidating political forces and groups, instilling fear and terror, and paralyzing their social activity or forcing them into behavior that aligns with the terrorist forces' objectives through brutal physical and psychological threats and destruction of people, groups, or property.

Terrorism has its socioeconomic causes in the property, class, and power relations of imperialism, the resulting antagonistic contradictions and their constant exacerbation, and the societal aggression, instability, and crisis nature that ensue. It is primarily used or exploited as a political strategy by the most reactionary forces of the bourgeoisie, often through imperialist intelligence services. Other social forces and groups outside the revolutionary workers' movement, particularly political, religious, and ethnic minorities, also use terrorism as a primary means to pursue their usually reactionary special interests, depending on their situation assessment. The application or exploitation of terrorism hinders, combats, or delays the progressive resolution of societal contradictions. This is true even when, in pseudo-revolutionary impatience, the resolution of societal contradictions is to be achieved abruptly through terrorist actions, or terrorism is seen as the only promising means for this goal. Therefore, terrorism objectively opposes social progress, primarily against socialism, its institutions, facilities, and citizens, against the working class, communist parties, and other progressive forces.

It endangers the development of socialist society and can complicate the struggle for peace, détente, and disarmament, strain relations between states, or initiate or support reactionary developments on a national and international scale. Terrorism as a social phenomenon is always the unity of political-ideological principles, direct actions (terrorist actions), concrete instruments for their implementation (terrorist means and methods), and active forces (terrorists). Its essential social basis is the petty bourgeoisie, which fluctuates due to social conditions and tends towards extremes, and from which the personnel base of terrorists mainly recruits. Other social forces and groups outside the revolutionary workers' movement also belong to the personnel reservoir. Terrorism is always politically and ideologically determined. It is ideologically stimulated, justified, and defended primarily by extreme variants of right-wing bourgeois, left-wing opportunist, and petty bourgeois ideologies, and by all forms of anti-communism and anti-Sovietism. Terrorist programs and actions mainly arise in the context of intense class battles in imperialist countries or globally, but also with the sudden emergence of partially intensified social contradictions.

The internationalization of social life worldwide, the global intensification of communication, especially the expansion of international aviation and electronic mass media, increase the impact and danger of terrorism. There are particularly close connections between terrorism and terror. Terror as a specific quality of concrete, real actions using violence is a part and concrete expression of terrorism when it is ideologically shaped by the theories that justify terrorism, arises from them, and aims to realize terrorism.

The appearance of terrorism, its actions, groups, and forces is diverse. For its political and political-operational analysis and assessment, the following criteria apply:

- Which class or social group employs terrorism, directly or represented by state or social institutions, for what goal, or exploits it for what goals?
- Are these goals directly or indirectly part of a political strategy or arise from it?
- What political and political-ideological justifications, legitimations, and explanations underlie terrorist actions, and what primarily motivates terrorists?

Based on this, the following essential forms of terrorism can be identified:

- Terrorism that is directly part of the subversive struggle of imperialism, sometimes created, controlled, or influenced by intelligence services, primarily targeting socialist states, their borders, foreign facilities, leading representatives, and other citizens and institutions.
- Terrorism of right-wing extremist, particularly neo-Nazi and neo-fascist forces and groups,
- Left-wing extremist, especially anarchist terrorism,
- Terrorism that appears as an accompanying phenomenon in the anti-imperialist struggle of peoples for national and social liberation.

The differentiated combat of all forms of terrorism is a societal task in which the MfS must play a decisive role.

Tipper

Persons acting on behalf of imperialist intelligence services, who, due to their objective and subjective possibilities and abilities, are purposefully used by the intelligence services to search for and select suitable persons for intelligence purposes.

Tipper can be both citizens of the home country and persons from the target country of subversive activities. Particularly those who undertake official or private travel to the target countries of the intelligence services, especially socialist states, or persons with legal positions, connections, and contacts in the target countries (e.g., diplomats, correspondents, employees of other institutions, representations, and organizations, corporate representatives, etc.) are used as tippers.

Tipper are differentiated in the investigation and recruitment of the persons they identify. The term tipper is primarily used by the Federal Intelligence Service (BND) and, in its interpretation, by other intelligence services. There is no clear distinction between tippers and other agent categories. Reliable couriers, → recruiters, → handlers, etc., can function as tippers.

Unofficial Collaborator (IM)

Citizens of the DDR or foreigners who have declared their willingness to cooperate conspiratorially with the MfS out of positive social conviction or other motives to reliably protect social development from all subversive attacks of the enemy, to comprehensively ensure the internal security of the DDR, and to further strengthen the socialist state community. The IM are the main forces of the MfS in the fight against the enemy. According to the various functions of the IM, the priority political-operative tasks to be solved by them, and the resulting requirements, the following IM categories are distinguished:

→ IM for political-operative penetration and securing of the area of responsibility (IMS),

→ IM of the defense with enemy contact or for direct processing of persons suspected of enemy activity (IMB),

→ IM for leading other IM and secret employees (FIM),

→ IM for special deployment (IME),

→ IM for ensuring conspiracy and communication (IMK).

The recruitment of IM and cooperation with them is carried out according to the official regulations and instructions of the MfS.

Unofficial Collaborator (IM) Candidate; Recruitment Conversation

Verbal influence by the operational employee on the candidate for IM with the aim of achieving their willingness for informal cooperation with the MfS and having them declare it in the form of a commitment. In preparation for the recruitment conversation, the → recruitment basis should be determined, the argumentation and tactics based on it, the design of the commitment, and the content of the initial tasks should be determined and documented in the → recruitment proposal. The dispute over the decision in each recruitment conversation requires persuasive work to achieve the desired goal by linking it with the candidate's personal needs, interests, and aspirations, thus creating motives for declaring willingness for informal cooperation. This requires:

- targeted and persuasive argumentation tailored to the candidate's individuality,
- clarity about the demands and expectations placed on the candidate and the consequences associated with their decision,
- objective and trust-building reactions to the candidate's critical points, reservations, concerns, etc.,
- the right choice of external conditions that guarantee the candidate's conspiracy and positively influence their decision.

Unofficial Collaborator (IM) of the Defense with Enemy Contact or for Direct Processing of Persons Suspected of Enemy Activity (IMB)

IM who works directly on persons engaged in enemy activities or suspected of enemy activities, gain their trust, penetrate their conspiracy, and, based on this, gain knowledge of their plans, intentions, measures, means, and methods, develop operationally significant information and evidence, and solve other tasks to combat subversive activities and counter the conditions and circumstances that favor them. The deployment of the IM of the defense with enemy contact is primarily aimed at penetrating the conspiracy of enemy agencies and forces and directly processing persons suspected of enemy activities according to Guideline 1/76.

Unofficial Collaborator (IM); Assignment

A politically-operative task assigned by the IM-leading employee to the IM for conspiratorial acquisition of specific information and evidence and for implementing preventive and damage-preventing measures. The assignment is derived from the individual → deployment direction of the IM and current political-operative tasks of the service unit. Each assignment must:

- be concrete, comprehensible, and tangible for the IM,
- be feasible,
- serve the education and capability of the IM and deepen their ties to the MfS,
- be largely verifiable in its fulfillment and usable for the continuous verification of the IM.

The assignment must include provisions and orientations regarding:

- the content of the action or performance to be realized by the IM,
- the scope of action applicable to it,
- the appropriate or required procedure while maintaining conspiracy and secrecy.

The realization of the assignment significantly depends on thorough consultation with the IM, qualified instruction, and careful development of the behavioral line. Each assignment must, therefore, be carefully prepared (→ meeting preparation).

The assignment can be given orally or, especially for complex and significant tasks, in writing. An exact record of all assignments must be kept in the IM's file.

Unofficial Collaborator (IM); Honesty

A personality trait of the IM characterized by features of sincerity, truthfulness, and integrity in word and deed concerning fulfilling the requirements set by the operational employee. This is expressed in truthful reporting about the actions and statements of persons or other significant findings, adherence to instructions, and willingness to share important statements about their own person. Significant factors influencing the development of honesty include the quality of the trust relationship with the operational employee, the IM's conviction of the necessity of the MfS's conspiratorial activities, and the IM's level of political-ideological attitudes and convictions. Honesty excludes behaviors of deception or deliberate misleading and is not equated with naive communicativeness or undifferentiated, offensive, or tactless "sincerity."

Unofficial Collaborator (IM); Prelude

Term for

1. The clarification and verification, conspiratorial contact, and development of the recruitment proposal for a candidate for IM registered in Department XII. The goal of working with the IM's prelude is to prove the candidate's actual suitability, reliability, and willingness for informal cooperation to solve political-operative tasks.

2. The file issued by Department XII, mainly documenting the political-operative necessity of recruiting the candidate, the intended deployment direction and category, the requirement profile, the circumstances of developing the initial hint about the candidate, plans for clarification and verification, the recruitment proposal, and other results achieved while working with the IM's prelude. The file is maintained according to official regulations and instructions.

Unofficial Collaborator (IM); Recruitment

1. Systematic, priority-oriented, qualitative supplementation and expansion of IMs, which must be carried out as an essential part of political-operative work, both currently and prospectively according to the political-operative situation in the area of responsibility.
2. Specifically, recruitment encompasses all measures for selecting and developing candidates for IM, their recruitment, and proving themselves as IM in the first phase of cooperation.

It is necessary to further strengthen work against the enemy and preventive, damage-preventing work, concentrating on the reliable protection of social development, ensuring the comprehensive internal security of the DDR, and strengthening the socialist state community. The fundamental goal of recruitment is to recruit people as IM who, based on the specific target and task to be solved, are objectively and subjectively able to significantly contribute to increasing the social effectiveness of political-operative work according to the specified quality criteria. Recruitment must ensure that people with suitable prerequisites for fulfilling these tasks mainly acquire operationally significant information, bring about socially and politically-operative useful changes, maintain the connection between current political-operative tasks and prospective security requirements, and preserve and enhance the internal security among the IMs. This requires constantly increasing the responsibility of leaders, middle management, and all IM-leading employees for planned, conspiratorial, and effective implementation of all individual measures to find people, evaluate them according to requirements, mobilize them, and involve them psychologically correctly in political-operative work.

Specific sub-tasks of recruitment include planning recruitment measures based on assessing the political-operative situation and determining the requirements, i.e., developing the specific requirement profile, developing initial materials from all operational processes and results, selecting candidates, recruiting them as IM (sometimes re-recruiting), and developing the newly recruited into fully deployable IM. The systematic processing of the IM's prelude, aimed at proving the candidate's suitability, reliability, and willingness for informal cooperation, includes the conspiratorial clarification and verification of the candidate, the conspiratorial contact, and the development of the recruitment proposal. Recruitment must create or expand the candidate's willingness for informal cooperation with the MfS and lead to their decision. The candidate's strong bond with the MfS must be developed, and their verification continued under the specific conditions of recruitment. The IM must be committed in such a way that the principal requirements for future informal actions, the associated obligations, the binding nature of the agreements made, and the implementation of initial tasks are expressed and effective. Based on the assessment contained in the report on the recruitment, the informal cooperation moves into the first phase, concluding the recruitment.

Bringing about the candidate's decision for informal cooperation with the MfS. Achieving the willingness and the resulting positive decision is the result of targeted influence to create the necessary motives in the candidate. During the gradual introduction of the candidate to recruitment, this influence extends over several contact discussions, including involving initial political-operative demands and tasks, while in the case of immediate recruitment, it primarily focuses on the recruitment conversation itself.

The recruitment basis should be determined in preparation for the recruitment conversation, and the argumentation and tactics based on it, the design of the commitment, and the content of the initial political-operative tasks should be determined. These provisions should be documented in the recruitment proposal.

The results of the recruitment and the resulting consequences for cooperating with the new IM should be detailed in the report on the recruitment.

Unofficial Collaborator (IM); Reparation and Reinsurance Motives

→ Recruitment bases that, as driving forces and efforts, arise in candidates for IM from their desire to avert negative consequences of norm violations committed or to compensate for damages caused by their actions. Prerequisites for this are objective facts and the recognition and experience of guilt. They are producible if facts exist that serve as compromising material, making the candidate aware of the norm violation, addressing their conscience, arousing guilt feelings, creating insecurity, and utilizing their moral and legal consciousness for positive compensatory actions. While reparation motives are based on genuine efforts, reinsurance motives may be more directed towards personal goals. In cooperation with such IM, other motives should be created simultaneously to ensure long-term, secure, and stable conspiratorial work.

See also Compromat

Unofficial Collaborator (IM); Stocktaking

Purposeful and targeted analytical work to assess the effectiveness of working with the IM.

The stocktaking is part of the → operational situation assessment in the area of responsibility and must be implemented at all management levels.

The main content of the stocktaking is the comparison between the current and future political-operative objectives and tasks in the area of responsibility and the quality, quantity, structure, and dislocation of the IM's stock.

The most important indicators for this are the criteria for high social and political-operative effectiveness of working with the IM (→ quality criteria).

The stocktaking serves to develop realistic decision-making bases

- for further intensifying work with the IM, their qualified education and capability,
- for the qualitative development and expansion of the IM's stock, especially in priority areas and among the target groups of the enemy,
- and for deploying the IM's stock according to security requirements, its appropriate structuring and dislocation.

The stocktaking must be carried out through periodic preparation of partial and overall assessments in the area of responsibility and the continuous, direct assessment of the IM and their operational work results in the daily work process.

Version

A statement based on operational information with a probability character that explains certain aspects of an operationally significant matter. Versions contribute to determining the direction and way of examining or further processing operationally significant matters, including the necessary politically operative measures.

The main aim of working with versions is to enable a purposeful and accelerated politically operative processing of operationally significant matters. Working with versions is an integral part of processing → operational processes, investigating politically operative occurrences, conducting operational → searches, and more.

Versions must be established primarily on those aspects of the operationally significant matter whose clarification is particularly important for successful processing, such as:

- The nature of connections of operationally processed individuals,
- The timing of the triggering of an operationally significant occurrence,
- The possible perpetrator or group of perpetrators when processing state crimes,
- The whereabouts of wanted persons or items.

For establishing versions, verified operational information must be available. Each version must relate to the specific matter. All versions resulting from the underlying operational information must be established and consistently verified. The verification of each established version must continue until it can be confirmed or refuted by corresponding facts.

Warning Levels

Agreed-upon behaviors in the intelligence communication system between the center and agents, triggered by → warning signals. Warning levels can encompass one or several consecutive behaviors (e.g., temporarily ceasing work, ceasing work and relocating materials, ceasing work and destroying materials, etc.).

Warning Signal

Signals used in the intelligence communication system, whose transmission from the center to the agent or vice versa triggers certain pre-agreed behaviors to ensure conspiracy until revoked.

As warning signals, inconspicuous objects, circumstances, acoustic signals, or visually perceivable signs adapted to normal life but clearly recognizable as warning signals to the recipient are used (e.g., certain postcards, missed telephone calls with a code word, changes in objects at the meeting place, etc.).

See also: Warning Levels

Who-Knows-Who Scheme (WKW)

A graphical representation of the connections of IM (informal collaborators) to individuals and these individuals among each other to timely recognize dangers that may arise from these connections for maintaining the conspiracy and security of the IM. The WKW scheme is also an orientation for the comprehensive utilization of the IM.

The prerequisite for this is the comprehensive identification of the IM's connections, their continuous supplementation and specification. Symbols are used to denote connections of different characters. The WKW scheme is also used in the processing of → operational processes to represent extensive operationally significant connections of suspects.

Work on the Enemy

The entirety of all politically-operative processes, measures, and actions within the framework of the defensive and intelligence work of the MfS in the DDR and the operational area, directly serving the goal of

- penetrating hostile agencies, secret services, institutions, organizations, groups, and factions,
- obtaining information about the plans, intentions, measures, means, and methods of the enemy,
- detecting and timely dismantling or disorienting hostile agencies, secret services, institutions, organizations, groups, factions, bases,

and hostile individuals through appropriate operational measures or preventing, restricting, or paralyzing their activities. In the defensive work of the MfS, case processing is the most immediate form of work on the enemy.

Young Cadres

Members of the MfS who, due to their excellent work results, exemplary behavior both on and off duty, knowledge and skills, and existing and potential leadership qualities, are systematically prepared and tested for inclusion in the → cadre reserve for senior positions and for assignment to a senior position. Junior cadre members are young personnel without a leading function. The work with junior cadres is defined within the main tasks of cadre work in the cadre program and plan of the respective service unit. It is also purposefully designed based on individual plans for education and training, with the involvement of mentors.

Youth; Analysis of Movements and Concentrations

A method of political-operative work that obtains operationally significant information about the composition, activities, and concentration points of rowdy, negatively decadent, and other criminally endangered young persons, groups, or groupings. Their actions and behaviors disturb order and security, posing a risk of subversive misuse by enemy forces.

Youth; Operational Diversion

A set of political-operative measures applied to rowdy, negatively decadent, and other criminally endangered young individuals or groups with the goal of deterring them from attending important social events and encouraging them to attend other events of lesser social or local significance.

Youth; Operationally Interesting Grouping

Both unstable and relatively stable associations of young individuals whose actions and behaviors, due to their negatively decadent, socially inappropriate, or socially dangerous, especially rowdy nature, disturb order and security and pose a risk of subversive misuse by enemy forces. This includes associations of young individuals suspected of enemy actions and those vulnerable to enemy misuse. The danger of such groupings is particularly influenced by the respective active influencers or ringleaders within them, who may themselves be subject to enemy influence or can be misused in a hostile manner.

Zionist Organizations

Reactionary, nationalist, racist, counter-revolutionary, anti-socialist, and anti-Soviet political associations that, based on Zionist ideology such as chauvinism, racism, and expansionism, are used by reactionary imperialist circles to escalate the international situation, incite anti-Sovietism and anti-communism, and combat the socialist states and the national liberation movement.

The organizational center of international and national Zionist organizations from 67 countries is the Zionist World Organization (WZO). The highest body of the Zionist World Organization is the Zionist World Congress, which meets every 4 years and elects the Zionist General Council and the Jewish Agency. The Jewish Agency is the permanent working body of the Zionist World Organization; it has offices in New York and Jerusalem.

The Jewish Agency has 12 departments, such as the Propaganda Department, the Immigration Department, and the Espionage/Intelligence Department. It is assumed that Zionist organizations are misused by the Israeli intelligence service and that there is close cooperation between the Israeli intelligence service and the Jewish Agency.

Abbreviation and Acronym Guide

Abs. Absatz
Section

Abt. n Abteilung Spionageabwehr in einer Bezirksverwaltung des MfS
Department of Counterintelligence in a District Administration of the MfS

Abt. VI Abteilung Passkontrolle / Tourismus in einer Bezirksverwaltung des MfS
Department of Passport Control / Tourism in a District Administration of the MfS

Abt. VIII Abteilung Beobachtung, Ermittlung, Festnahmen in einer Bezirksverwaltung des MfS
Department of Surveillance, Investigation, Arrests in a District Administration of the MfS

AG Arbeitsgruppe, kleinste Struktureinheit des MfS
Working Group, Smallest Structural Unit of the MfS

AKG Auswertungs- und Kontrollgruppe
Analysis and Control Group

BfgA Bundesanstalt für Gesamtdeutsche Aufgaben
Federal Agency for All-German Tasks

BfV Bundesamt für Verfassungsschutz
Federal Office for the Protection of the Constitution

BGP Bayerische Grenzpolizei
Bavarian Border Police

BGS Bundesgrenzschutz
Federal Border Guard

BKG Bezirkskoordinierungsgruppe
District Coordination Group

BND Bundesnachrichtendienst
Federal Intelligence Service

BRD Bundesrepublik Deutschland
Federal Republic of Germany

BV Bezirksverwaltung (des MfS)
District Administration (of the MfS)

BV/V Bezirksverwaltung/Verwaltung
District Administration

CIA Central Intelligence Agency (Auslandsaufklärungsdienst der USA)
Central Intelligence Agency (Foreign Intelligence Service of the USA)

CSSR Tschechoslowakische Sozialistische Republik
Czechoslovak Socialist Republic

DA Dienstanweisung
Service Instruction

DVP Deutsche Volkspolizei
German People's Police

EDV Elektronische Datenverarbeitung
Electronic Data Processing

EG Einführungsgesetz
Introductory Law

ELOKA Elektronische Kampfführung
Electronic Warfare

FIM Führungs-IM (IM zur Führung anderer IM und GMS)
Leading IM (IM for Leading Other IMs and GMS)

GBl. Gesetzblatt
Law Gazette

GKOS Geheime Kommandosache
Secret Command Matter

GKP Geheimschrift Kopierpapiere
Secret Writing Copy Papers

GMS Gesellschaftlicher Mitarbeiter für Sicherheit
Social Security Employee

GSE Grenzschutzeinzeldienst
Border Protection Service

GSSD Gruppe der sowjetischen Streitkräfte in Deutschland
Group of Soviet Forces in Germany

GT Geheimtinten
Secret Inks

GUST Grenzübergangsstelle
Border Crossing Point

GVG Gerichtsverfassungsgesetz
Court Constitution Law

GVS Geheime Verschlusssache
Secret Classified Matter

GVS-p Geheime Verschlusssache – persönlich
Secret Classified Matter - Personal

GZD Grenzzolldienst
Border Customs Service

HA Hauptabteilung (selbständige Diensteinheit im MfS)
Main Department (Independent Service Unit in the MfS)

HA I Abwehrarbeit in NVA und Grenztruppen
Counterintelligence Work in NVA and Border Troops

HA VI Paßkontrolle, Tourismus, Interhotels
Passport Control, Tourism, Interhotels

HA/V Hauptabteilung/Verwaltung
Main Department/Administration

HV Hauptverwaltung
Main Administration

HV/V Hauptverwaltung/Verwaltung
Main Administration

HVA Hauptverwaltung Aufklärung
Main Reconnaissance Administration

IM Inoffizieller Mitarbeiter
Unofficial Employee

IM-Vorlauf Mit dem IM-Vorlauf wurde in einem Untersuchungs- und Kontrollverfahren geprüft, ob sich die Anwerbung einer Person für das MfS lohnen würde
In the IM Preliminary Process, it was Checked in an Investigation and Control Procedure whether the Recruitment of a Person for the MfS would be worthwhile

IMB IM der Abwehr mit Feindverbindung bzw. zur unmittelbaren Bearbeitung im Verdacht der Feindtätigkeit stehender Personen

*Counterintelligence IM with Enemy Contact or for Immediate
Processing of Persons Suspected of Enemy Activity*

IME IM für einen besonderen Einsatz
IM for a Special Mission

IMK/DA IM zur Sicherung der Konspiration und des
Verbindungswesens/Deckadresse
IM for Securing Conspiracy and Communication/Cover Address

IMK/DT IM zur Sicherung der Konspiration und des
Verbindungswesens/Decktelefon
IM for Securing Conspiracy and Communication/Cover Phone

IMK/KO IM zur Sicherung der Konspiration und des
Verbindungswesens/Konspiratives Objekt
IM for Securing Conspiracy and Communication/Conspirative Object

IMK/KW IM zur Sicherung der Konspiration und des
Verbindungswesens/Konspirative Wohnung
*IM for Securing Conspiracy and Communication/Conspirative
Apartment*

IMS IM zur politisch-operativen Durchdringung und Sicherung des
Verantwortungsbereiches
*IM for Political-Operational Penetration and Securing the Area of
Responsibility*

INPOL Datenerfassungs- bzw.-übertragungssystem
Data Collection and Transmission System

JHS Juristische Hochschule Potsdam
Law University Potsdam

JURIS Datenerfassungs- bzw.-übertragungssystem
Data Collection and Transmission System

KD Kreisdienststelle des MfS
District Office of the MfS

Kfz Kraftfahrzeug
Motor Vehicle

KGB Komitet gosudarstwennoi besopasnosti (russ.): Komitee für Staatssicherheit
Committee for State Security (Russian)

KgU Kampfgruppe gegen Unmenschlichkeit (Berlin-West)
Combat Group against Inhumanity (Berlin-West)

KI Kriminalistisches Institut
Criminalistic Institute

KK Kerblochkartei
Index Card File

KPdSU Kommunistische Partei der Sowjetunion
Communist Party of the Soviet Union

Kripolis Kriminalpolizeiliches Informationssystem
Criminal Police Information System

KSZE Konferenz für Sicherheit und Zusammenarbeit in Europa
Conference on Security and Cooperation in Europe

LBK Lebender Briefkasten
Dead drop

Linie VI Arbeitsrichtung Paßkontrolle, Tourismus, Interhotels auf zentraler und Bezirksebene
Direction of Passport Control, Tourism, Interhotels at Central and District Level

Linie VIII Arbeitsrichtung Beobachtung/Ermittlung auf zentraler und Bezirksebene
Direction of Surveillance/Investigation at Central and District Level

LKW Lastkraftwagen
Truck

MdI Ministerium des Innern
Ministry of the Interior

MfS Ministerium für Staatssicherheit
Ministry for State Security

MI Militärinspektion
Military Inspection

MVM Militärverbindungsmission
Military Liaison Mission

NADIS Nachrichtendienstliches Informationssystem
Intelligence Information System

NATO North Atlantic Treaty Organization

NfD Nur für den Dienstgebrauch
For Official Use Only

NTS Nazionalno-Trudowoi Sojus (Emigrantenorganisation)
National Labor Union (Emigrant Organization)

NVA Nationale Volksarmee
National People's Army

OD Objektdienststelle
Object Service Office

ODH Operativ Diensthabender

Operational Duty Officer

OES Operativer Einsatzstab
Operational Task Force

OLZ Operatives Leitzentrum
Operational Control Center

OPK Operative Personenkontrolle
Operational Personal Control

OTA Ordnung zur Technologie der Kontrolle und Abfertigung sowie zur Arbeitsorganisation
Order for Control and Processing Technology as well as Work Organization

OUN Organisation Ukrainischer Nationalisten
Organization of Ukrainian Nationalists

OV Operativer Vorgang
Operational Procedure

OWVO Ordnungswidrigkeitenverordnung
Administrative Offense Regulation

PKE Paßkontrolleinheit
Passport Control Unit

PKO Paßkontrollordnung
Passport Control Regulation

RGW Rat für gegenseitige Wirtschaftshilfe
Council for Mutual Economic Assistance

Richtlinie 1/76 Richtlinie zum Führen Operativer Vorgänge zur systematischen Überwachung „feindlich negativer Kräfte"

Directive 1/76 for Leading Operational Procedures for the Systematic Surveillance of "Hostile Negative Forces"

RSD Rundspruchdienst
Broadcast Service

SOUD System (sozialistischer Länder) der vereinigten Erfassung von Informationen über den Gegner (russ.)
System of Socialist Countries for Unified Collection of Information about the Enemy (Russian)

StGB Strafgesetzbuch
Criminal Code

StPO Strafprozeßordnung
Code of Criminal Procedure

TBK Toter Briefkasten
Dead Drop

TIR Transport International de Marchandises par la Route
International Road Transport

TV Teilvorgang
Subprocess

U-Mitarbeiter Unbekannter Mitarbeiter
Unknown Employee

UdSSR Union der Sozialistischen Sowjetrepubliken
Union of Soviet Socialist Republics

UfJ Untersuchungsausschuß freiheitlicher Juristen (Berlin-West)
Investigative Committee of Freedom Jurists (Berlin-West)

UV-Lampe ultraviolettes Licht ausstrahlende Lampe
UV Lamp (Ultraviolet Light Lamp)

V-Leute Vertrauensleute, Verbindungsleute
Confidential Informants, Liaison Agents

VD Vertrauliche Dienstsache
Confidential Service Matter

VEB Volkseigener Betrieb
Publicly Owned Enterprise

VP Volkspolizei
People's Police

VPG Volkspolizeigesetz
People's Police Law

VSH-Kartei Vorverdichtungs-, Such- und Hinweiskartei
Pre-Consolidation, Search, and Indication Card Index

VVS Vertrauliche Verschlusssache
Confidential Classified Matter

WKW-Übersicht Wer kennt wen? - Übersicht
Who knows who? - Overview

WZO Zionistische Weltorganisation
World Zionist Organization

Z. u. A. Ziel- und Aufgabenstellung
Target and Task Definition

ZAIG Zentrale Auswertungs- und Informationsgruppe
Central Analysis and Information Group

ZEVIS Datenerfassungs- bzw. Übertragungssystem
Data Collection and Transmission System

ZFOV Zentraler Feindobjektvorgang
Central Enemy Object Process

ZK Zentralkomitee
Central Committee

ZKG Zentrale Koordinierungsgruppe
Central Coordination Group

ZOPE Zentralnoje Objedinenije Poslewojennych Emigrantow
Central Association of Post-War Emigrants

ZOV Zentraler Operativer Vorgang
Central Operational Process

ZPDB Zentrale Personendatenbank
Central Personal Database

ZZ-Arbeit Zweiseitige Zusammenarbeit (UdSSR - DDR)
Bilateral Cooperation (USSR - GDR)

Printed in Great Britain
by Amazon